P.146, line 5
Those playwri͏̈   came to
be known as "psychologists", whereas Vishnevsky and his
colleagues were known as "monumentalists". /1/

FIFTY YEARS ON:

GORKY AND HIS TIME

edited by

Nicholas Luker

ASTRA PRESS

1987

Astra Press

20 Candleby Lane, Cotgrave

Nottingham NG12 3JG England

Copyright 1987:   by Astra Press

All rights reserved. No part of this publication may be reproduced, stored in any retrieval system, or transmitted in any form or by any means, electronic, mechanical, photocopying or otherwise, without the prior permission in writing of the publishers.

ISBN   0-946134-09-X

CONTENTS

Editor's Preface   vii

The Young Gorky in Russian Literature of the 1890s.   1
BETTY Y. FORMAN

Gorky the Dramatist: A Re-Evaluation.   39
BARRY P. SCHERR

Vsevolod Garshin and the Early Gorky: Some Artistic and   63
Cultural Links and Affinities.
PETER HENRY

"Children of the Sun": A Drama of Unplaced Sympathies.   105
CYNTHIA MARSH

Gorky, Nietzsche and God-Building.   127
EDITH W. CLOWES

Death and Revolution: Gorky's "Egor Bulychov and the Others".   145
ROBERT RUSSELL

Games Tramps Play: Master and Man in Gorky's "Chelkash".   163
ANDREW BARRATT

Name Index   193

EDITOR'S PREFACE

> "I beg you to remember, once and for all, never join *any* party. Be what you are, an artist. That will be quite sufficient".
>
> *Maksim Gorky to Fedor Chaliapin in the early 1900s.**

This collection of articles derives from a proposal made by Monica Partridge and Garth Terry of the University of Nottingham to commemorate the fiftieth anniversary of Maksim Gorky's death in 1986.

It was felt that whilst Soviet research into very many aspects of Gorky's work has been both prolific and exhaustive during the last half-century, scholars in the West have devoted much less attention to it than it deserves. The point is underlined by the surprisingly short list - just twenty-eight titles in all - of published monographs and unpublished dissertations on Gorky given in Garth Terry's comprehensive recent bibliography, *Maxim Gorky in English: A Bibliography 1868-1936-1986* (Astra Press, 1986). In short, Gorky has been neglected here and so has faded from public view. It is hoped that the present collection will help to remedy this situation. Though the articles contained in it are intended primarily for Slavists, an attempt has been made to tailor them for the non-specialist who is interested in Russian literature of the period. Accordingly, for example, titles of works and all quotations are given in English.

The edition of Gorky's works normally used is the recent Soviet Academy

---

*Quoted in *Chaliapin: An Autobiography as Told to Maxim Gorky*, tr. and ed. Nina Froud and James Hanley (London, 1976), p.29.

EDITOR'S PREFACE

publication, *Polnoe sobranie sochinenii* in twenty-five volumes (Moscow, 1968-). However, as this edition does not include Gorky's letters, reference is sometimes made instead to the earlier *Sobranie sochinenii* in thirty volumes (Moscow, 1953).

Given the immense extent and variety of Gorky's work, it has proved impossible for reasons of space to include in this volume articles representative of all aspects of his writing. The collection does not pretend to discuss, for example, his long novels, memoirs or non-literary works, but focuses instead chiefly on his short prose and his dramas.

Betty Forman's essay, which opens the collection, sets the early Gorky as a writer and personality in the literary context of the late 1800s. Explaining how he carefully cultivated his special image so as to distinguish himself markedly from his contemporaries and to achieve national readership, the article surveys the genres used in his early prose. It concludes by examining the criteria affecting the choice of stories included in his first prose collections, published in 1898 and 1899. Barry Scherr's paper re-examines Gorky's status as a dramatist and investigates his less well-known plays of the early 1900s. It shows the development of his dramatic technique, pointing to the influence on him of other writers - notably Dostoevsky and Ibsen - and demonstrates how far he improved as a playwright by 1915. Peter Henry's essay traces the links between Gorky and his older contemporary Vsevolod Garshin (1855-88). It analyses Gorky's little-known early story about insanity, "A Mistake" (1895), revealing the circumstances surrounding its genesis and drawing comparisons between it and Garshin's powerful tale "The Red Flower" (1883). Cynthia Marsh examines what is probably the most neglected of all Gorky's plays - *Children*

EDITOR'S PREFACE

of the Sun — which received its premières in both Moscow and St. Petersburg in 1905. After touching on the differences between the two productions, the paper investigates the ideological ambiguities inherent in the work and attempts to clarify Gorky's own sympathies in it.

In her very different article, Edith Clowes addresses the vexed question of Nietzsche's influence on the development of Gorky's *Weltanschauung*. The essay explains that while Gorky eventually appeared to overcome his philosophical mentor in the myth of "God-building" illustrated in his prose works *Confession* (1908) and *Childhood* (1913), the collectivist social myth which he evolved remained in many ways aesthetically close to Nietzsche. Robert Russell's paper explores Gorky's late play *Egor Bulychov and the Others* (1931) and investigates differences between its Moscow and Leningrad productions. Describing the difficulties encountered by the various actors in interpreting the role of Bulychov, the essay compares the drama with Tolstoy's story "The Death of Ivan Il'ich" (1886) and suggests that, concerned as he was with the philosophical problem of death, Gorky probably had Tolstoy's tale in mind when writing the play. The volume concludes with Andrew Barratt's article which examines Gorky's celebrated early story "Chelkash" (1895) in detail, showing the various unsatisfactory critical interpretations of the work and exploring the ambiguity central to Gorky's treatment of his hero.

I wish to thank the contributors to this collection for the consideration and courtesy which they have shown me as editor in agreeing to my suggestions. Nowhere, I hope, have I done violence to their original texts. I would also like to thank my friend and colleague Garth Terry, Slavonic Librarian at the University of Nottingham, for his scrupulous accuracy and

EDITOR'S PREFACE

care in making the final drafts and for his expert advice at all stages of the work. Finally, I wish to express my gratitude to my son Nathaniel for the unfailing patience and understanding that he has displayed towards me during the many hours which I have spent preparing this volume.

Nottingham, England　　　　　　　　　　　　　　　　　　NICHOLAS LUKER
February, 1987

THE YOUNG GORKY IN RUSSIAN LITERATURE OF THE 1890s

Betty Y.Forman

Harvard University,

Massachusetts, U.S.A.

(i) Russian Literature in the 1890s

By 1890 Russian writers and critics felt that their literature had reached an impasse. The 1880s, known as the *bezvremen'e* ("difficult times"; period of social stagnation), reflected the political climate of quiet despair following the monarchy's crackdown on radical activity after the assassination of Alexander II in 1881. In literature, lyric poetry had withered under the depredations of utilitarian criticism. Prose fiction, especially in its longer forms, had gone into either decline or eclipse due to the withdrawal or deaths of the most prominent writers. In 1881 Dostoevsky had died after calling for a revival of literature based on dedication to truly Russian character types and Orthodoxy. Two years later Turgenev had died in France, while by 1887 Tolstoy, having experienced his "conversion", had virtually ceased writing novels and stories altogether, publicly dedicating himself instead to works of preaching, pedagogy and political commentary. In 1889 Saltykov-Shchedrin and Chernyshevsky, both representatives of the radical democratic tendency of the 1860s, had also died. Among younger writers who made their reputations in the 1880s, the most prominent disappeared tragically: Nadson died in 1887 while Garshin committed suicide in 1888. Such depressing events continued into the 1890s, when Gleb Uspensky went mad in 1892 and Leskov died largely unrecognised in 1895. In the West, Nietzsche, by now insane, was sequestered for the rest of his life, triggering the first wave of international interest in his work, an interest which soon reached Russia. Extraliterary events, such as the Volga famines of 1891-92 and the attendant cholera epidemics, contributed first to the general malaise and then to a call for activism. Readers and critics alike noticed the abdication or loss of writers and the dearth of good literature, and awaited new tendencies in the arts, looking forward to the appearance of something strong and new.

In the early 1890s Russia experienced a general interest in philosophies of individualism: Western importations were foremost among them, especially Nietzsche, and to a lesser extent towards the century's end, Stirner, Ibsen and Strindberg. Nietzsche was a primary influence on writers of all ideological and aesthetic groupings, from right to left. In the ideological sphere legal Populism coexisted with rising Marxism, introduced into Russia by Plekhanov in 1882 with his pamphlet *Our Differences*, but neither tendency predominated.

In literature all modernising trends coexisted and were represented by writers of different "schools" or "tendencies". The differentiation of Symbolists and Decadents from Neo-Realists had begun, but the schools were not as yet clear-cut. Certain themes and stylistic characteristics, however, seemed common to all: individualism, self-assertion, spiritual quest, chiliasm, Prometheanism, impressionism and an interest in lyric poetry or in short prose forms. The sharp differentiation between Neo-Realists and Symbolists became complete by the turn of the century with the formation of literary circles around notable writers possessing strong personalities and clear aesthetic programmes.

The theoretical expectations of significant writers at the end of the

THE YOUNG GORKY

1880s and the beginning of the 1890s reflect the moods shared by their readers and can be considered as manifestos calling for the amelioration of Russian literature. They predict the developments of the 1890s - general modernising tendencies, idealism, impressionism, the amalgamation of the realistic and romantic, and the growing split between Neo-Realism and Symbolism. A short account of the views of Korolenko, Chekhov and Merezhkovsky will show the dominant tone of their thinking.

Korolenko, literary editor of the influential Populist "thick" (*tolstyi*) journal *Russkoe bogatstvo*, reported on his editorial practice in unpublished personal journal entries of the late 1880s in which he outlined his expectations for a new literature. Himself a writer of prose sketches and "autobiographical" fiction, he was not at home with poetry and eschewed "poetical prose". He felt that Russian literature had been in decline since the 1860s and detected that decline in the poor quality of the unsolicited manuscripts which novices continually sent him. His own programme represented a revival of the concerns shown by democratic realism in the 1860s and 1870s - the unmasking of social evils and the expression of ethnographic and reformist interests - together with a new kind of romanticism, the striving after an ideal of social amelioration and the full realisation of human potential. He rejected naturalism, preferring a synthesis of realism and romanticism along the lines of his own fiction./1/ Heroic and everyday interests would coexist in a work whose protagonist, taken from real life rather than from fantasy, would act against the background of the masses and their interests as well as his own. Korolenko preferred prose narratives - especially accounts in the first person and legends - to poetry. He felt strongly that literature had a teaching func-

BETTY FORMAN

tion, an obligation to criticise existing social evils and to present positive ideals that would inspire the reader. Indeed, as far as Korolenko is concerned, it seems not unfair to say that if Gorky had not existed, it would have been necessary to invent him. In fact, he had a hand in doing so, since his advice helped to shape Gorky's early works.

For his part, Chekhov, who had achieved prominence as a serious prose writer by the middle of the 1880s, also commented on the decline in the quality of Russian literature. In a brief but pithy letter to his editor, A.S.Suvorin of *Novoe vremia*, he set out his observations, which though rather unsystematic, can be taken both as a diagnosis and a set of recommendations for the future. Dissatisfied with his recently published "Ward No.6" (1892), he jokingly apologised for having provided "sweet soda water" where alcohol was wanted, and was not surprised that Suvorin, "a bitter drunkard", had noticed the difference and deplored it. Chekhov felt that he was typical of the writers of his generation in producing such "spiritless" works: "Tell me in all honesty", he wrote, "which of my contemporaries [i.e. men aged between 30 and 45] has given the world even a drop of alcohol - Aren't Korolenko, Nadson and all the current playwrights just soda water?"/2/ Weak writing, a sign of the times, he went on, was encouraged by utilitarian criticism and was indicative of a general sickness which Chekhov characterised as a loss of sexual potency. The real difference between great and merely good writers was that the latter lack "goals". Necessary ideals may be of two types: proximate goals linked with politics, or goals such as God, life beyond the grave, man's happiness, and answers to the classic "accursed questions" of Russian literature. The immanence of the overriding goal or ideal in the description of everyday

THE YOUNG GORKY

existence distinguished great literature from the literature of the moment, caught in the morass of *byt*. Instead of calling for "art for art's sake", Chekhov harked back to the same tradition of finding spiritual ideals in reality of which Korolenko approved, and for which Merezhkovsky, despite his reputation as an aesthete, also advocated at this time. Chekhov himself did not plan to change his own technique, and found the then modish suicidal despair as much out of place as deceiving himself with old or new ideals. He cited Nadson and Garshin as archetypal writers of the 1880s, martyrs to the sickness of the times, and like Korolenko, he looked forward to a literature of conviction and belief that he himself felt unable to produce.

It was D.S.Merezhkovsky, the early Symbolist poet and prose writer, who in his well-known essay "On the Reasons for the Decline and On New Tendencies in Contemporary Russian Literature" – first given as a series of public lectures in 1892 and then published in 1893 – produced the best statement on the perceived decline of Russian literature in this period. The essay reflects the early stage of his interests, an amalgam of Populist ideas and the nascent Symbolism which he would continue to develop. His promulgation of a religiously oriented Symbolism would seem to have aims contrary to those espoused by Korolenko and Chekhov, but his diagnosis and recommendations possess elements similar to theirs, and what he actually calls for, "a new idealism", bears great similarities with the aims put forward by his contemporaries.

Merezhkovsky felt that "poetry" was an extended sense, a God-given elemental force couched in the literary productions of individual human beings./3/ He rejected all forms of the dominant positivist and utilitarian criticism as unworthy of promoting an art whose beauty was to be beyond conventional morality. He diagnosed why good poetry was not being produced in Russia and what it would take to foster it, citing those writers who seemed to be working towards it. The lack of a common culture, the destructive effect of utilitarian criticism, growing ignorance, and the ruin of the Russian language all contributed, he felt, to the decline. Especially guilty was the "petty press" (*melkaia pressa*), the newspapers and minor journals which fostered bad, sensational writing and were the dominant means of entry into literature for hordes of semi-educated men risen from the people - "the democratic journalistic Bohemia",/4/ as he called it. The debasing of literature to a trade whose system of honoraria enslaved writers, and the established route to national literary recognition - first, by publication in the *melkaia pressa*, then in the central "thick" journals, and only afterwards in collections in book form - spoiled the status of the book, he believed, making it a pale derivative of periodical publications.

So as to counter the opposing tendencies of the time, which to him were extreme materialism coexisting with passionate idealism, Merezhkovsky rejected literary positivism in favour of nascent Symbolism as a way of gaining knowledge of both reality and the ideal. But he felt that the symbols should flow naturally from the depths of reality rather than take the form of consciously generated dead allegories. Ideal poetry in the future would thirst for the unexpected, continually surprising the reader. As he saw it, the new art was to have three main elements: mystical content, symbols, and the expansion of artistic impressionability. Among previous Russian writers with these gifts, he believed, were Turgenev, Tolstoy,

THE YOUNG GORKY

Dostoevsky and Goncharov, all seemingly realistic writers who had gifts for fantasy, poetry and the portrayal of heightened passion, and who confronted the "accursed questions" of Russian life. Characters, too, could be symbols; he considered the contrast of opposing types as a deeply real symbolism.

Merezhkovsky found late Populism close to idealism, and thus valued Korolenko highly, especially his lyrical prose poem "Makar's Dream" (1885). For him it signalled the living spirit of Russian literature, touching as it did the spiritual life of the people. But he regarded most contemporary Russian writers as impotent martyrs, among them Garshin, whose one-volume posthumous collection he nevertheless lauded for its sincerity, dense language and perfection of form. In contrasting Chekhov with Garshin, he found one healthy and the other sick, but saw both as members of a generation characterised by frailty and the same ultimate spiritual limitations.

As Merezhkovsky saw it, the task facing Russian poets and prose writers was to develop a literature based on the idealism practised by their greatest immediate predecessors. From Goncharov new writers would learn sensitivity and impressionability, from Dostoevsky an interest in psychology, and from Tolstoy the search for new faith and truth.

Merezhkovsky's discussion not only set a goal for Russian literature but also clarified how publishing worked in the 1890s. Promising young men published stories and reports in provincial newspapers, then strove to be printed in the newspapers and "thick" journals of the capitals. Finally, when they had accumulated enough material, they would publish a collection of their best work in book form, often under the title *Sketches and Tales*

BETTY FORMAN

(*Ocherki i rasskazy*), as did Gorky, Korolenko, Chirikov, Bunin and many others./5/ The publication of their books depended on their previous appearance in print (and perhaps even suffered from it), but this sequence of steps was necessary to achieve a literary reputation of any stature. Unlike both Korolenko and Chekhov, however, who used it, Merezhkovsky rejected this dominant method of reputation-building, though he was unable to propose any alternative. His appeal for symbols arising from reality resembled the call for a blend of Realism and Romanticism that was so important to Korolenko's view in the late 1880s, and, like Korolenko, he showed a preference for such genres as allegories and legends.

Gorky's stories of the 1890s satisfy the recommendations made in these three typical appraisals of Russian literature on the threshold of the 1890s. While not pursuing any religious ideal, Gorky's idealistic characters, especially the authorial figure of Maksim, strive after as yet unattainable spiritual goals – the fulfilment of human potential and the exercise of boundless individual freedom. They have the forcefulness that Chekhov so misses in the work of older writers like Korolenko and himself. While Korolenko frowned on poetic prose (but himself wrote long nature descriptions), Merezhkovsky called for more "poetry", finding it even in Korolenko's "Makar's Dream". Early works of Gorky, including "Grandad Arkhip and Len'ka" (1894), "The Old Crone Izergil'" (1894), "Song of the Falcon" (1895), and even "Twenty-Six Men and a Girl" (1899) at the very end of the 1890s, are filled with it. The descriptions of nature so dear to Merezhkovsky in the works of Turgenev, Chekhov and Korolenko are also vital in Gorky's early prose, where nature not only decorates the action but also interacts with the characters in a truly symbolic way in which

THE YOUNG GORKY

natural phenomena are personified (for example, the industrialised harbour in "Chelkash" (1895), the inimical stormy landscape that kills "Grandad Arkhip and Len'ka", and the untamable river that Kirilka in the eponymous 1899 story can hold only temporarily at bay). Nature is also portrayed in the double-framed legends where contemplation of its beauty sets the scene for an appreciation of the spiritual content of the tales which Maksim's teachers tell him. Gorky's contrasting of symbolically opposed characters, especially in the stories which treat Maksim and his fellow-travellers, and in "Chelkash" and "Cain and Artem" (1899), also corresponds to Merezhkovsky's recommendations.

Gorky's early career also reflects Merezhkovsky's picture of what he considered the abuses of the contemporary system of publication. Gorky may be considered one of the "semi-educated, semi-cultured" members of the "democratic Bohemia" who rose through the deplored sequence of newspaper publication, journal issue and collection in book form. Moreover, his command of the Russian language might be viewed as imperfect, for his early stories mix dialect forms and frequent foreign intrusions with poetic prose and nature descriptions, all of which Gorky tended either to alter or eliminate in later editions of his work.

(ii) Gorky and the New Archetypes of the Writer as a Celebrity

In the 1880s a substantially new pattern for mass appreciation of the author as a literary celebrity emerged in Russia. The literary personality of a writer was based on the appeal made to broad sections of the reading public by his biography and personal style as well as by the content of his works. This type of reception differed in degree from that accorded to older and classical Russian authors, whose works tended to be read largely independently of the writer's personality. The process of formation of literary celebrity in this period was aided by technical devices such as the photograph and inexpensive means of reproducing it, cheaper and faster printing, and the commercial cultivation of a mass reading public drawn from all social classes and levels of literacy.

The first two writers to be received in this way were Garshin and Nadson. Formed in the atmosphere of the *bezvremen'e*, both their works and biographies are characterised by morbidity, dissatisfaction, disappointment, suicidal insanity and the frustrated yearning for a prophet. The posthumous glory of these young men was based on the peculiar appeal of their tragic lives, small *oeuvres* and personal charisma. The pattern persisted into the 1890s, making possible Gorky's success on the same basis of the connection between his life and work, though the actual quality of his fame differed fundamentally from that of his predecessors.

Vsevolod Garshin (1855-88) was a prose writer of noble stock whose works dramatised a conscience stricken by the inhumanity of war and the ills of modern urban society - specifically, rising capitalism and prostitution. His first significant story, "Four Days" (1877), an indictment of war which reflected his own experiences in the Russo-Turkish War of 1877, appeared in *Otechestvennye zapiski* that year and brought him fame. He continued to publish in this and other periodicals until 1888, when at the age of thirty-three he committed suicide by throwing himself down a staircase. The appearance of a slim volume of his collected works (he only finished about thirty stories) assured his continued fame, and he was

THE YOUNG GORKY

regarded as one of the foremost writers of the 1880s by both readers and colleagues. He was especially popular among the younger generation. His dark, unusual beauty was an important factor in his celebrity, and it inspired his friend Repin not only to paint his portrait but also to use him as the model for Ivan the Terrible's ill-fated son in his well-known painting "Ivan Grozny and his Son Ivan" of 1885.

Garshin's stories encompass only a few genres: allegories such as "Attalea Princeps" (1880) and "That Which Never Happened" (1882); exciting episodes in the lives of Petersburg artists and prostitutes, among them "An Event" (1878) and "Artists" (1879); tales of war and its aftermath ("Four Days" and "A Very Short Romance" (1878)); and explorations of insanity such as "The Red Flower" (1883). All are short stories, most of them first-person accounts by a narrator who is closely identified with his creator. Garshin's works retained their popularity and are still widely read because of their high quality and appeal.

Whilst the lyric poems of Semen Nadson (1862-87), which are of less literary worth, are no longer read, his contemporary popularity was greater than Garshin's. Nadson was the son of a half-Jewish government official and a mother from the noble Mamontov lineage. After losing both parents by the age of ten, he was sent to military school by relatives, where he proved sickly and weak. However, he began writing poetry very early, published his first verses at sixteen, and brought out his first collection in 1885. Five editions were published before his death, bringing him national recognition. When he died of tuberculosis in 1887 at the age of 24, he left no successor as leading civic poet. Already high, his popularity increased dramatically after his death, and he remained the

BETTY FORMAN

idol of Russian youth for many years. Like Garshin's prose, his poetry expresses the temper of the times: the pessimism of the disappointed "intellectual" (*intelligent*), thoughts on sickness, fear of insanity, disdain for the crowd and for rising capitalism, and the fruitless quest for a saviour. While he lived, Nadson gave public readings which boosted his popularity and closely linked his personality with his works. Indeed, it was early recognised that his reputation derived from the coupling of his biography and his writing. Korolenko's letter of 11 July, 1887 to a budding poet comments on the effect of this link between Nadson's life and works:

> I am certain that the greater part of Nadson's poems, if printed separately and under other names, would not produce the enchantment that these verses have on readers of the late poet... The reader knew him in his individuality and grew to love a known personality... There appears a sort of unstated addition which might be termed a psychological aberration. The direct and immediate impression of a poem falls on prepared earth, widening the sphere of its influence, embracing previously received impressions and becoming enhanced by them./6/

Even Chekhov shared in the unusually high esteem felt by Nadson's contemporaries: "Nadson was a much greater poet than all contemporary poets put together...", he wrote.

Garshin and Nadson had much in common beside their short lives and limited *oeuvres*. Both were regarded as typical young "intellectuals" of the *bezvremen'e* and as secular martyr saints of Russian literature. Both were handsome, inspiring artists to paint them and admirers to buy their portraits on postcards and calendars. Each was physically weak and chronically sick with illnesses that had a long history of appeal in romantic literature. Each had exotic elements in his background, and each produced a small, easily mastered corpus of work homogeneous in genre which matched

THE YOUNG GORKY

the mood of contemporary Russian society. The close identification of the writer with his narrative or his lyrical consciousness facilitated the identification of the reader with the central character of a poem or story as well as with its author. Garshin's and Nadson's popularity during their lifetime was enhanced by the live performances at which both excelled. Both emphasised themes of passivity and loss of hope, as well as a frantic but fruitless search for teachers, prophets and inner peace. Both detested philistines, the crowd and capitalism. And both, well-known and much loved before their early deaths, achieved instant popularity on first publication, a popularity which grew to enormous proportions so that their posthumous fame only declined after many decades. Moreover, their initial appeal to youth quickly widened to include the whole reading population.

So it was that by the end of the 1880s there existed in Russia a clear pattern of identification between an author and his works, and of literary celebrity based on this identification. It was possible for the reader to follow and enjoy an author as a literary personality, to be concerned as much with his life as with his work, and, in a sense, to "read" his life and works together.

Gorky made use of this established pattern of appreciation in the construction of his narrator Maksim in his own self-presentation. In the 1890s the chief aim of Gorky's belletristic *oeuvre* was to develop this persona. He himself regulated his personal image so as to produce the maximum effect, using unique costume and bearing to differentiate himself both from other more conventional intellectuals as well as from ordinary workers and artisans. It did not matter that he was unusually tall, had thick, reddish, unruly hair, a distinctive low voice with the character-

BETTY FORMAN

istic, uncorrected broad "o" of his Volga accent, piercing blue eyes and an attractive, vital homeliness. His dress for all seasons and occasions was a conscious stylisation of that worn by the worker or peasant - the *kosovorotka* (Russian shirt), wide trousers, boots, and a broad-brimmed hat and wide cape for outdoor wear, but all made of rich leather or fabrics in seasonally appropriate colours./8/ He thus distinguished himself from the traditional literary intellectual, whose image was that of a self-effacing, neat, calm figure in his standard jacket and trousers.

The many photographs, portraits and caricatures of Gorky from the period 1890 to 1905 show variations of this costume. Several of the writers who became his disciples and co-workers - among them Andreev, Skitalets and Teleshov - also adopted his "uniform". Like Nadson, Gorky was tubercular, and like Garshin, he had attempted suicide. From his association with "vagabonds" (*bosiaki*) and his much-vaunted emergence from the "depths of life" that was reflected in his early autobiographical sketches, he knew the harsh reality of current events; while from the associations with exotic folk story-tellers and prophets described in his works, he was familiar with traditional myths and prophecies. But while details of Gorky's background and personal style recall Garshin and Nadson, the chief ingredients of the persona he constructed are contrary to theirs, and correspond to the expectations and mood of the 1890s. He satisfied the need felt by both readers and critics for a strong, self-assertive type in both the author and his characters, and he offered in himself and his narrator Maksim a vital, new intellectual to replace the prematurely exhausted, doomed young men of the 1880s.

In two short autobiographical works - his first - of the late 1890s,

THE YOUNG GORKY

Gorky laid the foundations of his life myth. In the earlier of the two, sent to the critic Vengerov for a projected critical-biographical dictionary, he stresses his brutalised childhood, his status as an autodidact and the succession of casual jobs and wanderings that preceded his literary début, which he then describes in detail. In a characteristically self-depreciating but commanding tone, he concludes with an estimation of his life and work in 1896:

> Until now I have written nothing that has pleased me, and for this reason I do not keep my pieces - ergo, I am unable to send you them. It seems there are no unusual events in my life, and it seems there never have been; besides, I don't clearly understand what it is customary to consider using these words./9/

The denial of the value of his works, his self-obfuscation, and his cavalier disregard for the astonishing life he has sketched - so very unusual for a Russian writer of his age - were calculated to interest and attract the reader. The second autobiographical sketch, first published in the journal *Sem'ia* in 1899, is similar, stressing his family background, early jobs and reading, first teachers (especially Korolenko), and his publication history./10/

At all stages of Gorky's career, self-creation was an important motif. Indeed, successful self-creation is the primary theme in the group of stories which depict Maksim in association with "vagabonds" or other "teachers of life". In other works of the 1890s, however, the self-creation of the major character, from Pavel of "The Miserable Creature Pavel" (1894) through Foma of *Foma Gordeev* (1898) to Pavel Lunev in "Three of Them" (1899), is always unsuccessful. The pattern of failed self-creation persists throughout Gorky's career, culminating in *The Life of Klim Samgin* (1927-36); the only exception is the monumental autobiographical trilogy *Childhood, Among People, My Universities* (1913-23), the great drama of self-creation in which Alesha Peshkov, the unwanted orphan, transforms himself into Maksim Gorky, the celebrated Russian writer. It is curious that Gorky did not finish this work, never taking it past his Kazan period when he was about twenty. To have taken Alesha from his "universities" along the path towards literary maturity would have meant revealing the largely self-conscious process of creation of a persona that Gorky elaborated in his life and works of the 1890s. His literary memoirs of 1910-24 are sketchy discussions of only a few aspects of this process such as associations with writers and the dynamics of provincial literary circles. Part of Gorky's fiction of the 1890s sympathetically observes the intelligentsia of his time - his colleagues. These are pitiful cases like the hallucinating, doomed friends of "A Mistake" (1894) and the alcoholic teacher Korzhik who knows his Nadson by heart in "Teacher Korzhik's Leisure Hours" (1896). But the most enduring part of it established the author's own persona as a vital new kind of "intellectual/vagabond" for the reader to emulate, to use as a model to supersede the type of the "man of the 1880s".

(iii) Gorky's Use of Genres in the Early Stories

Between the 1870s and the 1890s the centre of gravity in Russian prose shifted from the novel to shorter forms. Abandoned by great writers like Turgenev, Dostoevsky and Tolstoy, the novel became "standardised" as a form for the topical chronicling of Russian life by such secondary writers as Boborykin./11/ The "tale" (*rasskaz*) and "sketch" (*ocherk*) became the

THE YOUNG GORKY

representative genres of prose fiction. Free from the canons imposed on the longer forms, they became a field for experimentation in method./12/ Confusion of the "tale" and "sketch" led to use of the title *Sketches and Tales* (*Ocherki i rasskazy*) for many anthologies, including Gorky's./13/ The names of the genres were loosely applied so as to indicate the incompleteness of the artistic product and the author's intention that the work represented a larger picture which did not yet exist.

A "poetic consciousness of the world" was common to realistic literature at this time and it fostered an interest in other short forms such as myths and legends./14/ Additionally, the conditions of publication in journals and newspapers fostered a trend towards relative brevity as well as the increasing prominence of quasi-fictional genres. Korolenko, a "master of these forms", exerted a strong influence on the younger generation of writers./15/

Gorky's choice of genres was typical for his time. He produced "sketches", "tales" and similar types of stories with loose generic titles. Most of his best pieces are derivatives of the travel sketch. Anecdotes, legends and holiday stories were prominent features in the newspapers where he served his literary apprenticeship. Indeed, he did not write a novel until the end of the century, and that only after achieving fame as a writer of short forms. The same is true of his plays. Gorky's novels and plays are actually scenes of highly dramatic confrontations between pairs of characters, or between one character and a group, continuing the confrontation pattern for the structure of conflict that he developed in the stories.

BETTY FORMAN

(iv) Travel Tales: Aggrandising the Role of the Narrator

To the category of travel tale belong all the stories in which Maksim associates with "vagabonds", as well as several "vagabond" stories narrated in the third person such as "Friends" (1895) and "Chums" (1898). Primarily, these tales deal with Maksim and a fellow-wanderer whose accomplice he is. Unlike previous travel tales in Russian literature, however, the narrator does not sharply observe and criticise the people he meets, nor does he primarily diagnose the ailments of the land he sees; instead he simply learns from his fellow-wanderers whilst sharing their lives. Even travel tales without the "vagabond", such as "The Little One" (1895), in which Maksim travels with a peasant couple and is inspired by their retelling the life-story of a dead girl Populist, and "Kirilka" (1899) where he witnesses the grandeur and misery of the Russian peasant in conflict with nature, have this characteristic function of educating the narrator. In his association with scoundrels like Shakro in "My Fellow-Traveller" (1894) and Promtov in "The Rogue" (1898), picaresque elements appear when he is used by these dubious acquaintances. Ultimately he learns much, even from such rascals, becoming cleverer than they are and turning their exploitative slyness to his own advantage as a would-be writer and teacher As a group these stories may be said to function together as a kind of novel of vocation and education for the narrator. The physical movement of the journey parallels his maturation as a man and artist, for it is a movement through psychological as well as physical space.

THE YOUNG GORKY

(v) Legends

Legends are an important genre in Gorky's fiction of the 1890s. The sources of his legends are characteristic: they are reputedly told by exotic prophets or poets among the non-Russian peoples of the Empire, or they derive from Western sources. The subjects of the legends deal with the assertion of the individual personality and the value of illusion for life, both of which are key themes for the writer. The best are the three double-framed legends written between 1892 and 1895. They are central to the creation of Gorky's philosophy and literary persona, and were included in his collected works. Amid an exotic landscape Maksim meets a venerable teacher who tells an inspiring legend or two, and in so doing, communicates his or her mission to the young man. "Makar Chudra" (1892) contains the gypsy legend of Loiko and Radda; "The Old Crone Izergil" the legends of Larra and Dan'ko; and "The Song of the Falcon" the Tatar Ragim's tale of the Falcon and the Snake. The latter is not properly a legend but an allegory or animal fable, with a structure and function resembling those of the other two stories. Although Soviet scholars have searched ethnographic collections for the antecedents of all these legends, originals from folk sources have not been found.

Single-framed or unframed legends are also important and have sources in exotic folklore - for example, "The Khan and his Son" (1896) and "The Mute" (1896) - or in printed works about the medieval West. All appeared in newspapers in 1895 and 1896, but curiously enough, Gorky chose none of the six he wrote in the 1890s for his collected works.

BETTY FORMAN

(vi) Mood Pieces

Plotless mood pieces are a minor part of Gorky's work in the 1890s. All appeared in newspapers where they were a standard item. "The Fair at Goltva" (1897), for instance, chosen for the second volume of his collected works, conveys the sights and sounds of a Ukrainian fair and was highly regarded by Chekhov, Tolstoy and Korolenko, the latter wishing that Gorky would write more stories in this vein.

(vii) Anecdotes

Anecdotes that concern readers and writing are important in this period because they demonstrate Gorky's view of the writer's mission and show him in conflict with his reader. The piece "The Reader" (1898) is the best and was reprinted in his collected works. Those anecdotes which do not concern writing and literature are very poor. All are short pieces published in newspapers in 1896 and were never collected by Gorky.

(viii) Animal Fables and Allegories

Apparently Gorky wrote animal fables very early under the influence of Shchedrin, but destroyed or lost most of his early items. In the form of confrontations, animals who stand for social classes or particular world-views compare their philosophies. The most famous, "The Siskin Who Lied and the Woodpecker Who Spoke the Truth" (1893), which contrasts active and passive approaches to life, is Gorky's best allegorical tale, a central text on the value of illusion for life. Others in his work of the 1890s

THE YOUNG GORKY

are either unfinished or weak, and he selected none of them for his collected works.

(ix) Holiday Stories

As a reporter for *Volgar'*, *Samarskaia gazeta* and *Nizhegorodskii listok* in the 1890s, Gorky wrote fifteen holiday stories, a minor genre which appeared in the holiday numbers of newspapers. These tales are usually short, playful (full of dream sequences, apparitions and chronological shifts), and are appropriate to the holiday in question. Often written at short notice, they show evidence of haste and lack of care. Mood pieces are typical of this genre, as are framed narratives with dream sequences and surprise endings. There are four categories of holiday stories: New Year stories (*novogodnie rasskazy*) tend to be prospective in outlook, embodying resolutions for the future or drawing attention to social wrongs requiring correction in the coming year. Gorky wrote two of these, neither of which he included in his collected works. Christmas stories (*sviatochnye rasskazy*), overlapping in their chronology with New Year stories, appeared during *sviatki*, the twelve days between Christmas and Epiphany (January 6), and including *Kreshchenie*, the eve of Epiphany. These stories, inspired by the folk customs of fortune-telling (*gadanie*) practised on Epiphany Eve, stress dreams, tricks of fate, the intrusion of the past and future into the present, and instances of the supernatural. "The Driver" (1895) and "An Apparition" (1896) are Gorky's stronger tales of this type. In both he pushed beyond generic limitations to inject a theme and philosophy consonant with the preoccupations of his less tailored

BETTY FORMAN

work, critiques of the intelligentsia and the merchant class. The critique of the petty bourgeoisie (*meshchanstvo*) in "About the Devil" (1899), and the aesthetic and programmatic discussion of "More About the Devil" (1899), are both less successful, as is "Songs of the Dead" (1900). Christmas stories (*rozhdestvenskie rasskazy*) appeared on Christmas Day. Sentimental and emotionally manipulative, they often featured children whose miserable existence was terminated by death and immediate reception into heaven. Gorky's first and best story of this type, "The Girl and Boy Who Did Not Freeze to Death" (1894), may be regarded as an anti-Christmas story, a successful transposition of the prevalent minor key of patient suffering typical of such stories, into Gorky's major key of protest and vitalism. Accordingly, in this work a homeless brother and sister successfully beg and steal a Christmas feast.

Gorky's Easter stories (*paskhal'nye rasskazy*) acknowledge the alternation of Death and Resurrection, the advent of spring, and the cyclical nature of life. Perhaps more than the others, they suited his predilection for forceful characters and natural beauty. His three Easter tales, "On the Rafts" (1895), "The Bell" (1896) and "The Quarrel" (1899), are powerful productions characteristic of Gorky's early manner. In fact, "On the Rafts" is one of his finest stories of any period.

At its best, Gorky's use of the holiday genre shows his ability to manipulate its conventions for the benefit of his own art and to breathe his own kind of life into tired clichés. In their attempt to achieve a clear form, these pieces are unlike most of his other tales, with their unenlightening, purposely "careless" subtitles and genre attribution (episode/ sketch/from life), as well as the frequent intrusion or constant presence

THE YOUNG GORKY

of the narrator or a surrogate.

(x) Collecting and Anthologising: Gorky's Public *Oeuvre*

By the end of the 1890s Gorky had available for possible collection 128 pieces of short prose. Varied in theme and genre, they provided the basis for his selections for the collected works *Sketches and Tales*, issued in two volumes in 1898, and in a second edition with a third volume in 1899 (see Tables I-III). The selection made by Gorky and his publishers does not proportionally replicate the contents of the whole corpus of stories and it is worth investigating why. With the publication of the first two volumes, Gorky instantly established his reputation and national popularity. These stories, along with the visible persona which he had created, fostered a view of him as a self-made man from the "depths" and affected the mass reading public as no Russian writer had ever done before, though as shown above the careers of Garshin and Nadson provided a prototype for the close link between personality and art. In determining which stories to collect in the first two volumes, Gorky strove to make himself as appealing as possible and inclined towards stories already published in the central press ("thick" journals and weekly newspapers) and towards the more significant tales published in provincial newspapers.

A veteran of provincial papers in Tiflis, Samara, Nizhny Novgorod and Odessa, Gorky had work published in national journals of all political persuasions. His début in the central press came in *Russkoe bogatstvo*, the organ of legal Populism edited by Mikhailovsky and Korolenko, when he was a *protégé* of the latter; but he also published in the legal Marxist jour-

23

nals *Novoe slovo* and *Zhizn'* and in the liberal *Russkaia mysl'*, *Kosmopolis* and *Zhurnal dlia vsekh*. His choice of outlet in this period seems to have been opportunistically rather than ideologically motivated, since he also published three times in *Severnyi vestnik*, by 1897-98 considered the leading early Decadent and Symbolist journal. In all, during the period from 1892 to 1899 it seems unjustified to assign him to a particular political niche: he was not yet a Marxist, though he was possibly moving in that direction. In about 1902 he joined the Social Democrats, and later became a fellow-traveller of the Bolsheviks.

Gorky first mentioned the possibility of collecting his stories for publication to Korolenko in a letter of October, 1895, claiming that the firm of Priashnikov had proposed issuing a volume that at that time could only have included newspaper stories and "Emel'ian Piliai" and "Chelkash", both of which had appeared in the central press. But Gorky refused, thinking it too early for such an enterprise./16/ In late 1897, though, at the time of the forced closure of *Novoe slovo* - to which he had contributed "Heartache" (1896), "Konovalov" (1897) and "Creatures That Once Were Men" (1897) - he wrote to its editor Vladimir Posse to ask whether his stories were worth collecting. He sent clippings of the following works: "Once in Autumn", "On the Rafts", "Makar Chudra" and "The Fair at Goltva", all powerful pieces which had appeared at least once in provincial newspapers and journals. Posse saw the potential value of the stories and presented the clippings to the publisher O.N.Popova, whose firm issued primarily non-fiction with a Populist tendency. At first Popova agreed, but then changed her mind, for, as she told Posse: "To publish Gorky would be like throwing money away: no one will buy his stories, for even Bunin's stories

THE YOUNG GORKY

don't sell, and he's incomparably more talented than Gorky"./17/ Two other publishers also refused because of lack of funds and the presumed lack of readership for an obscure provincial beginner. Sadly, even Gorky's colleagues in the publishing co-operative "Znanie" ("Knowledge") refused too. Finally, a friend S.P.Dorovatovsky and his associate A.P.Charushnikov, a steamboat inspector and old Populist activist, agreed to issue the work. Its success was to mark the start of an enterprise which lasted until 1914./18/ Between March 24 and 31, 1898, Volume I of Gorky's *Sketches and Tales* appeared in an edition of 3,000 volumes, and between April 16 and 23, Volume II was issued in an edition of 3,500. By August he was considering the selection for his third volume, which appeared between September 1 and 8, 1899, along with a second edition of the first two.

Each of the three volumes contained ten stories, all previously published at least once. Broadly speaking, the first two were evenly divided between stories that had appeared in provincial papers and those issued in central journals. Thus in Volume I five stories came from journals and five from newspapers. Five "vagabond" stories, with "Chelkash" placed first, were included, all striking works ranging from "romantic" to "realistic" types, with "Makar Chudra" and "On the Rafts" complementing "The Orlov Couple" and "Grandad Arkhip and Len'ka". The legend "The Song of the Falcon", related to "Makar Chudra" in structure and theme, was the only story in its category of legend to be included. Of the rest, "Heartache" deals with the spiritual crisis of a merchant, "The Trickster" (1897) with the conflict between an artisan and an intellectual, and "Zazubrina" (1897) and "For Want of Anything Better to Do" (1897) with the tensions between an individual and the group which victimises him. Each of these stories is based on the structural principle of "confrontation" (*stolknovenie*) or contains episodes of confrontation. In addition, four of the ten pieces feature the narrator-persona Maksim (Table IV summarises these characteristics).

In Volume II five of the stories had first appeared in periodicals and six in newspapers. (Ten tales were included in each edition of Volume II, but Gorky used "The Siskin Who Lied..." as the key story in the first edition, substituting the realistic "Boles'" in the second). But the newspaper stories included such powerful works as "The Affair of the Clasps", "The Old Crone Izergil'" and "Boles'". Seven of them concern the "vagabond", including the legend "The Old Crone Izergil'", and again they range from the romantic and mythical ("Mal'va") through the sentimental ("Emel'ian Piliai") to the realistic or naturalistic ("In the Steppe", "Creatures Who Once Were Men" and "The Affair of the Clasps"). Seven pieces feature Maksim as narrator (six of the "vagabond" stories and "Boles'"). In addition, one tale, "The Mistake", concerns the intelligentsia, and one, "The Fair at Goltva", is a much-praised mood piece. All the stories except "Emel'ian Piliai" and "The Fair at Goltva" are confrontational in form.

In Volumes I and II ten tales are from 1897, six from 1895, and the rest from 1892 to 1894. Most of the newspaper stories written for *Samarskaia gazeta* and *Nizhegorodskii listok* during 1895 and 1896 were excluded, and the themes developed in them - the intelligentsia, the petty bourgeoisie, the merchant class and children - would remain unknown to people reading Gorky's works only in these early collections.

The profile of these volumes suggests that Gorky and his publishers in-

THE YOUNG GORKY

tended to present him as a writer about "vagabonds" who knew them through intimate contact, and who sought to acquaint his readers with an attractive narrator-protagonist who would appear in his programmatic stories as an advocate of individualism and protest against society and man's fate. Critique of the intelligentsia *is* featured, but this motif appears secondary. The stories chosen depend upon themes and structures of confrontation They are dramatic and lively and contain nature descriptions and dialect, though not cumbersome linguistic stylisation.

Gorky's initial criteria for choosing the tales for Volume III were different, and because of surviving published correspondence, we know more about them. Towards the end of the 1890s, wishing to diversify his appeal from that of a writer about "vagabonds", he wrote the long story about the intelligentsia, "Varen'ka Olesova", first published in *Severnyi vestnik* in 1898, then returned to his old newspaper clippings, intending Volume III to be something new that would concentrate on the intelligentsia. According to his correspondence with Dorovatovsky in 1898 and 1899, he wished "that the whole third volume be filled with stories of the petty intelligentsia. Let's see how I'll do in that sphere"./19/ Some months later he claimed: "Maybe the third volume will have less beauty, but more substance"./20/ From this correspondence it is clear that the choice of stories for the collected works was made by Gorky himself, Dorovatovsky and Posse, and that the final volume had a shape other than that first envisaged by Gorky. Unfortunately, only his correspondence with Dorovatovsky has been published, but even that gives a clear idea of the criteria affecting the third volume and how they changed as the work progressed and decisions were taken.

BETTY FORMAN

In its published form Volume III contains ten stories, as did both its predecessors. Five treat the "vagabonds" - about the same proportion as in the previous two volumes: "Cain and Artem" which is a last attempt to mythologise the "vagabonds"; "My Fellow-Traveller" and "The Rogue", depicting Maksim's conflict and experiences with "vagabond" teachers of life; and the realistic "Chums" and "Once in Autumn", the latter an urban variant of the "vagabond" tale dealing with Maksim and a young prostitute. The programmatic stories "About the Devil", "More About the Devil" and "The Reader" combine a critique of the petty bourgeoisie with a programme for literature, and as such deal with the intelligentsia. However, it is only "Varen'ka Olesova", the long story placed first in the volume, which deals with intellectuals of all types and fulfils the original intention which Gorky had for the book. Varen'ka herself is an impossible "wild girl" who has more in common with the "vagabonds" of the less realistic stories which deal with them ("Hollyhock" (1897), for example), but she serves as the touchstone for the pretensions of the other characters. "Kirilka" portrays the peasant in conflict with the merchant, intellectual and bureaucrat, a conflict observed through the eyes of Maksim. In all, seven of the stories contain Maksim as a character ("Cain and Artem", "Chums" and "Varen'ka Olesova" are narrated in the third person), and all, except for "About the Devil" and "Once in Autumn", are strongly confrontational. Eight of them were written in 1898 or 1899, while "My Fellow-Traveller" and "Once in Autumn" appeared in *Samarskaia gazeta* in 1894 and 1895 respectively. It is clear that the tales about "vagabonds" with Maksim as a participant narrator continue to predominate in this collection. The ultimate decision made by Gorky, Dorovatovsky and Posse was to

THE YOUNG GORKY

continue in the vein established by the first two volumes and so reinforce Gorky's reputation as a writer of autobiographical "vagabond" stories and other tales of confrontation. The material included in this third volume was mainly recent and consisted primarily of work already published in central journals. The continued decision not to choose stories about the intelligentsia, merchant class and peasantry, however worthy they were, masks the true frequency of occurrence of those themes and makes Gorky's image as a celebrant of the "vagabond" deceptively clear-cut in a way that is not supported if one examines the whole corpus of his work during the 1890s. The "vagabond" tales which present Maksim as either exploiting the "vagabonds" or rejecting them - as in "At the Salt-Flat" (1893) and "Two Bums" (1895), for example - were not chosen for the collections.

The stories excluded from Volume III by Gorky form an instructive group and help to show how he chose to present himself. Of the intelligentsia tales, "Vengeance" (1893), which contrasts honour among Georgian mountain people with the low mores of peasants, and even worse, the urban intelligentsia, was rejected, as was the interesting "Suicide" (1895), with its confrontation between a suicidal intellectual and a prostitute, a piece which Gorky discarded as "an empty thing"./21/ "A Fairy Tale" (1895), the retelling of a middle-class woman's life and a crucial text for understanding Gorky's treatment of women, was also rejected, as was "The Lonely Man" (1896), the chilling story of an old nobleman's wait for death after a worthless life of self-indulgence. "A Dream" (1896), the internal debate of a young intellectual over the conflicting demands of self-preservation and love for another was initially to be included, as Gorky requested in May, 1899, together with "The Rogue" and "My Fellow-

BETTY FORMAN

Traveller", which illustrate the same conflict of interests, but it was eventually eliminated./22/ Thus these bitter little tales, all highly critical of the petty bourgeoisie and the pretensions of the intelligentsia, were excluded. Of the "vagabond" stories, "How They Caught Semaga" (1895), a sentimental piece, was excluded after some consideration, as was the naturalistic "Vas'ka the Red", a treatment of the life and death of a bouncer in a whorehouse which was not published until 1900 because of censorship problems. "Finogen Il'ich" (1899), a grudgingly admiring treatment of a strong peasant, was proposed by Gorky for inclusion, but was ruled out by May, 1899./23/ Of the stories dealing with illusion, the following were rejected: "The Chimney Sweep" (1896), about a chimney sweep killed by unrequited love; "A Girl" (1897) (the second part of "Crimean Sketches", 1897), on the need for hope, however illusory, in the face of death; and "A Beauty" (1896), about the crushing of the ideal of beauty by the realisation of the coarseness of reality, a work which Gorky approved but which Dorovatovsky rejected./24/ Thus the programmatic stories in the volume are "About the Devil" and "More About the Devil", which exhort the intelligentsia to live forthrightly, and the literary manifesto "The Reader", which directs the writer to educate, unmask evil and inspire his readers.

As a whole, therefore, Volume III was not the "transition to a new form of literary existence" that Gorky first envisaged,/25/ but a continuation in terms of theme and structure of the previous two volumes, and as such it reinforced and extended his reputation as a writer of "protesting heartache", as Posse called him. Only the specifically literary nature of

THE YOUNG GORKY

the programmatic stories and the elimination of the categories of legend and framed legend differentiated the third volume of the collection from the first and second.

As has been shown, Gorky's achievement of his reputation in the 1890s was an amazing piece of work for a young and inexperienced writer. He managed his career path so as to move rapidly from publishing first in provincial newspapers and then in the prestigious "thick" journals of the capitals, before finally winning national publication of a careful selection of his work that would assure him both unprecedented sales and popularity. His themes answered the call for forcefulness and idealism in literature made by such writers as Korolenko, Chekhov and Merezhkovsky, and he was able to create and manipulate a seductive, charismatic and very public personality which quickly brought him a following much greater than that of previously idolised writers such as Garshin and Nadson. This achievement of national fame through his life and work succeeded beyond Gorky's expectations in captivating his readers, and after seven years of careful work and planning, he had become a nationwide sensation. He then continued in search of further directions for his literary work as both writer and editor-entrepreneur. After 1899 he limited his output of short prose to only a few holiday pieces and programmatic legends per year, returning to the short story form later, notably in about 1910 when he started work on the *Through Russia* (1919) collection, and then in the 1920s. Consciously aspiring to the status of Dostoevsky or Tolstoy, he began to write full-length novels such as *Foma Gordeev* and *Three of Them*. Under the influence of Chekhov, he wrote his first plays, *The Petty Bourgeois* (1899) and *The Lower Depths* (1902), where his fascination with the "vagabond" found its apotheosis, before moving on to the later plays and novels which castigate the intelligentsia and merchants, and finally, to his autobiography.

NOTES

1. See V.G.Korolenko, *Polnoe posmertnoe sobranie sochinenii* (Poltava, 1925), Vol.1: *Dnevnik (1891-1893)*, p.97.
2. A.P.Chekhov, *Polnoe sobranie sochinenii i pisem v 30-i tomakh. Pis'ma v 12-i tomakh* (Moscow, 1977), Vol.5: *Pis'ma (mart 1892-1894)*, p.133.
3. D.S.Merezhkovskii, "O prichinakh upadka i o novykh techeniiakh sovremennoi russkoi literatury", in his *Sobranie sochinenii* (St. Petersburg, 1911), Vol.9, p.211.
4. *Ibid.*, p.2.
5. See letter from I.A.Gruzdev to Gor'kii, November, 1926, in *Perepiska A. M.Gor'kogo s I.A.Gruzdevym*, Arkhiv A.M.Gor'kogo, 11 (Moscow, 1966), pp.92-3.
6. Korolenko, *op. cit.*, pp.81-2.
7. Chekhov, *op. cit.* (Moscow, 1975), Vol.2: *Pis'ma (1887-sent., 1888)*, p.21.
8. A.E.Bogdanovich, *Stranitsy iz zhizni Maksima Gor'kogo* (Minsk, 1965), p.26, as quoted by L.M.Farber in his *A.M.Gor'kii v Nizhnem Novgorode* (Gor'kii, 1968), p.83.
9. M.Gor'kii, "Avtobiograficheskaia zametka 1897 goda", in S.A.Vengerov, *Russkaia literatura dvadtsatogo veka, 1890-1910* (Moscow, 1914), Vol.2, p.192.
10. See M.Gor'kii, "Avtobiograficheskaia zametka iz zhurnala *Sem'ia*", in S.A.Vengerov, *op. cit.*, pp.192-4.
11. See, for example, I.A.Dergachev, "Dinamika povestvovatel'nykh zhanrov russkoi prozy semidesiatykh-devianostykh godov XIX veka", in *Russkaia literatura 1870-1890 gody, vyp.9: Problemy tipologii realizma* (Sverdlovsk, 1976), p.7.
12. Dergachev, *op. cit.*, pp.13-14.
13. See Gruzdev, *op. cit.*, p.92.
14. Merezhkovskii, *op. cit.*, p.17.
15. J.Holthusen, *Twentieth Century Russian Literature* (New York, 1972), p.5.
16. See Gor'kii to Korolenko, letter of 3 October, 1895, in M.Gor'kii, *Sobranie sochinenii v 30-i tomakh* (Moscow, 1953-54), Vol.28: *Pis'ma, telegrammy, nadpisi, 1889-1906*, p.17.
17. V.A.Posse, *Moi zhiznennyi put': dorevoliutsionnyi period (1864-1917)* (Moscow-Leningrad, 1929), pp.144-5.
18. *Ibid.*, p.146.

19. Gor'kii to Dorovatovskii, letter of August, 1898, in Gor'kii, *op. cit.*, p.29.
20. Gor'kii to Dorovatovskii, letter of 18 October, 1898 - *ibid.*, p.33.
21. Gor'kii to Dorovatovskii, letter of April, 1899 - *ibid.*, p.72.
22. *Ibid.*, p.80.
23. *Ibid.*, p.79.
24. *Ibid.*, p.81.
25. Gor'kii to Dorovatovskii, letter of second half of June, 1899 - *ibid.*, p.87.

* * * * *

BETTY FORMAN

TABLE I
Sketches and Tales I: Dorovatovskii and Charushnikov, 1898

Title + Date Written	First Publication

1. Chelkash (August, 1894) — *Russkoe bogatstvo*, 1895, No.6 [journal]

2. Song of the Falcon (1894) — *Samarskaia gazeta*, 5 March, 1895 [newspaper]

3. On the Rafts (March, 1895) — *Samarskaia gazeta*, 2 April, 1895 [newspaper]

4. Heartache (February/March, 1895) — *Novoe slovo* (St. Pb.), 1896, No.9 (June), No.10 (July) [journal]

5. Zazubrina (1897) — *Zhizn' Iuga* (Odessa), 1897, No.18 [weekly]

6. Grandad Arkhip and Len'ka (Fall/December, 1893) — *Volgar'*, 13-23 February, 1894, No.18 [newspaper]

7. For Want of Anything Better to Do (1897) — *Samarskaia gazeta*, 25 December, 1897 [newspaper]

8. The Trickster (end 1896) — *Severnyi vestnik* (St. Pb.), 1897, No. 8 [journal]

9. Makar Chudra (September, 1892) — *Kavkaz* (Tiflis), 12 September, 1892 [newspaper]

10. The Orlov Couple (1896-97) — *Russkaia mysl'* (St. Pb.), 1897, No.10 [journal]

THE YOUNG GORKY

TABLE II
Sketches and Tales II: Dorovatovskii and Charushnikov, 1898

	Title + Date Written	First Publication
1.	Konovalov (November/December, 1896)	*Novoe slovo* (St. Pb.), 1897, No.6 March [journal]
2.	Mal'va (1897)	*Severnyi vestnik* (St. Pb.), 1897, Nos. 11 and 12 [journal]
3.	The Fair at Goltva (July, 1897)	*Nizhegorodskii listok*, 20 July and 3 August, 1897 [newspaper]
4.	The Woodpecker Who Lied and the Siskin Who Told the Truth (end 1892)	*Volzhskii vestnik*, 4 September, 1893 [newspaper]
4a.	Boles'* (1897)	*Nizhegorodskii listok*, 1 May, 1897 [newspaper]
5.	The Affair of the Clasps (1895)	*Samarskaia gazeta*, 2 and 7 July, 1895, [newspaper]
6.	Creatures that Once Were Men (1897)	*Novoe slovo* (St. Pb.), 1897, No.1 (October), No.2 (November) [journal]
7.	Emel'ian Piliai (1892-93)	*Russkie vedomosti*, 5 August, 1893
8.	The Old Crone Izergil' (September, 1894)	*Samarskaia gazeta*, 16-27 April, 1895 (3 parts) [newspaper]
9.	In the Steppe (Spring, 1897)	*Zhizn' Iuga* (Odessa), 1897, Supplement 1 [newspaper]
10.	The Mistake (1894)	*Russkaia mysl'* (St. Pb.), 1895, No.9 [journal]

* replaced "The Woodpecker..." in 2nd ed., 1899

BETTY FORMAN

TABLE III
Sketches and Tales III: Dorovatovskii and Charushnikov, 1899

Title + Date Written   First Publication

1. Varen'ka Olesova   Severnyi vestnik (St. Pb.), 1898, Nos.
   (1896-97)   3,4,5 [journal]

2. Cain and Artem   Mir bozhii (St. Pb.), 1899, No.1
   (Fall, 1898)   [journal]

3. Chums   Zhurnal dlia vsekh, 1898, No.10 [jour-
   (July, 1897)   nal]

4. Once in Autumn   Samarskaia gazeta, 20 and 22 July,
   (end 1892)   1895 [newspaper]

5. Kirilka   Zhizn' (St. Pb.), 1899, No.1 [journal]
   (end 1898)

6. About the Devil   Zhizn' (St. Pb.), 1898, No.1 [journal]
   (Fall, 1898)

7. More About the Devil   Zhizn' (St. Pb.), 1899, No.2 [journal]
   (January, 1899)

8. My Fellow-Traveller   Samarskaia gazeta, 11-13 December, 1894
   (1894)   (6 parts) [newspaper]

9. The Rogue   Nizhegorodskii listok, 1 February, 1898,
   (Spring, 1897)   "A Meeting with Him", 1st part, [news-
                                           paper]
                                           Zhizn', 1898, No.15 (May) and No.16
                                           (June), complete in 3 chapters [jour-
                                           nal]

10. The Reader   Kosmopolis (St. Pb.), 1898, No.11
    (1895/1898)   [journal]

THE YOUNG GORKY

TABLE IV
Themes and Structures of Stories for *Sketches and Tales I-III*

Theme	Volume	Title
Vagabond	I:	Chelkash(c); On the Rafts(c); Grandad Arkhip and Len'ka(c); Makar Chudra(*c); The Orlov Couple(*c)
	II:	Konovalov(*c); Mal'va(c); The Affair of the Clasps(*c); Creatures that Once Were Men(*); Emel'ian Piliai(*); The Old Crone Izergil'(*c); In the Steppe(*c).
	III:	Cain and Artem(c); Chums(*c); Once in Autumn(*); My Fellow-Traveller(*c); The Rogue(*c).
Allegory/Fable	I:	Song of the Falcon(*c).
	II:	The Woodpecker Who Lied...(*c); Boles'(*c).
	III:	About the Devil(*c); More About the Devil(*c); The Reader(*c).
Peasant	III:	Kirilka(*c).
Merchant	I:	Heartache(c).
Crowd vs. Individual	I:	Zazubrina(*c); For Want of Anything Better to Do (c).
Intelligentsia	I:	The Trickster(c).
	II:	The Mistake(c).
	III:	Varen'ka Olesova (c).
Mood Piece	II:	The Fair at Goltva.

* with Maksim as participant-narrator
c Confrontation (*stolknovenie*) form

37

GORKY THE DRAMATIST:

A RE-EVALUATION

Barry P.Scherr

Dartmouth College,

New Hampshire, U.S.A.

The one play, indeed the one work, that assures Gorky's continuing international reputation is *The Lower Depths*. It was an immediate success when first staged by the Moscow Art Theatre in 1902 (with such well-known actors as Kachalov and Moskvin – to say nothing of Olga Knipper, Chekhov's wife, and Maria Andreeva, soon to become Gorky's common-law wife, in the female leads – and with Stanislavsky himself playing the role of Satin). Ever since, it has rarely been off the Russian stage and has received frequent productions throughout Europe and the United States. The more serious playgoer in England and America is also, of course, likely to be familiar with at least several other plays by Gorky: *The Petty Bourgeois* (also translated as *The Philistines*) (1902), *Summerfolk* (1904), *Enemies* (1906), and *Egor Bulychov and Others* (1932). This list includes several works from Gorky's first years as a playwright (the period from 1902 to 1906) and one, *Egor Bulychov*, written towards the very end of his career.

Missing here, though, and rarely, if ever, performed for the benefit of English-speaking audiences, are the plays that Gorky wrote from about 1910 into the World War I years. This period witnessed some of his finest writing: the last of his early novels, the unjustifiably ignored (at least in the West) *Life of Matvei Kozhemiakin* (1910-11); the first two-thirds of

39

BARRY P. SCHERR

his autobiographical trilogy, *Childhood* (1913) and *In the World* (1916); and the fine sketches that comprise the collection *Through Russia* (1912-1917). For some reason the plays that Gorky wrote during this period have largely fallen from view, yet they are hardly without interest. At the very least they mark an attempt to break away from his earlier dramatic work both in structure and in theme. Indeed, it is possible to argue that as a group the final plays from the 1910s, in their probing of characters' psychology and in their unadorned yet intense plots, represent Gorky's finest writing for the stage.

This is not to say that his earlier plays are bad or to deny *The Lower Depths* its place as his pre-eminent single work for the stage. However, in their generally large casts of characters and often less than perfect structure, the early works serve as a prime example of the "disunity" that Gorky seems to have cultivated at times in his writing. He tends to strive for density over clarity and for chaos over order. Characters may come and go, while plot lines may suddenly disappear or emerge from an apparent void. This is equally true of his novels and stories. Gorky was not averse to creating finely-wrought tales, such as his well-known "Twenty-Six Men and a Girl" (1899), but more often than not he would ignore niceties of form in order to pack all his thematic concerns into a work. In the more successful stories, such as "Creatures That Once Were Men" (1897), based, like "Twenty-Six Men and a Girl", on his adventures as a youth in Kazan, all the disparate elements eventually coalesce to create a powerful effect; in others, though, the diffuseness only leaves the reader confused.

The Lower Depths is perhaps the prime example of a work that is an acknowledged masterpiece and yet contains several seemingly glaring

GORKY THE DRAMATIST

weaknesses that would be enough to destroy a lesser play. For instance, at least some of the characters do not seem to be entirely necessary. The Baron, the Actor, Bubnov, and the locksmith Kleshch are all dwellers within the lower depths. Gorky manages to create individualised figures out of each of them, yet the play would clearly be easier for audiences to follow had he combined these four figures into one or two, and the story-line would have remained intact. More critically, the characters who are most important for the play's intrigue - the thief Vaska Pepel, Kostylev, owner of the lodging-house where the action takes place, and Kostylev's wife and sister-in-law - have relatively little to do with the play's philosophical concerns. In turn, the characters through whom Gorky develops the conflict in world-views that lies behind the play's thrust - most notably, Luka and Satin - stand somewhat apart from the rest of the work's action. Chekhov was perhaps the first to note another serious flaw in the play's structure - the absence of nearly all the stronger characters from the fourth and final act./1/ More recently, the Russian critic L.M.Farber has discerned three distinct plays within this one work: the four-act main play about the lower depths themselves and those who inhabit them; a philosophical drama in acts one to three that deals with questions of good and evil, of the truth versus the "consoling lie"; and a one-act political play in act four, an authorial monologue presented through Satin. Indirectly accepting Chekhov's critique, Farber notes that the links among these three "plays" are essentially weak./2/

Yet in *The Lower Depths* the various elements finally fuse into a work that achieves greatness. No doubt part of the reason lies in Gorky's talent for drawing characters who simply play well on the stage. Luka, the

BARRY P.SCHERR

Actor, Nastia, Vaska Pepel and the Baron are all original creations who are clearly individualised and create powerful impressions. The very types of people whom Gorky chose to portray may also help to account for the work's success. Strikingly, of all his plays only here are the vagabonds and failures "on the bottom" his main subject. Such figures were central to his stories from the start, but the play seems to have marked an apotheosis of the theme and served as an at least temporary farewell to it; /3/ only when he turned to his autobiographical writings some years later did he revive his interest in such figures. In any case, he avoided the vagabond type in his later plays, which certainly have some well-drawn characters, but they lack the uniqueness that makes this play so special. Furthermore, the figure of Luka, whom Gorky at least in his subsequent writings was at pains to single out as a negative character, a person with a harmful influence on others, is probably the first of his great creations for the stage. The way in which Luka is played and the degree to which he is made broadly sympathetic can have a telling effect on the message conveyed by the play's first three acts./4/ The chief theme associated with Luka, the battle between "truth" and the "consoling lie" - and indeed the struggle among various kinds of "truth", some of which are destructive - helps unite the work. Through Luka Gorky poses an ethical question that is perhaps insoluble and has continued to fascinate audiences ever since the play's first performance. Thus the strength and originality of the secondary figures, the creation of a strange yet powerful central character, the very exotic quality of the lower depths that Gorky depicts, and the complexities of the play's theme largely account for its deserved success.

Even though Gorky's other plays from his early period have often

GORKY THE DRAMATIST

received effective stagings both in Russia and abroad, on the whole they are less impressive as literary works. They exhibit some of the faults found in *The Lower Depths* but lack its offsetting strengths. Rather than dealing with the bottom of the social order, they depict Russia's middle and upper middle class - a milieu familiar enough from Chekhov's plays. Indeed, Gorky's *The Petty Bourgeois* bears many resemblances to *The Three Sisters*, a play premièred the year before this 1902 work, while *Summerfolk* contains at least vague echoes of *The Seagull* (1896). A comparison of the two writers immediately reveals Chekhov's relative economy and efficiency. Take, for instance, Gorky's *Summerfolk*. The play has both a writer, Shalimov, and a would-be writer, Kaleria, the sister of the lawyer who represents all that is worst in the lives of these *dacha* dwellers. They are roughly analogous to Chekhov's Trigorin and Treplev. Riumin, a formerly lively individual who now fears all that life offers, fails ignominiously when he tries to shoot himself, an episode reminiscent of Treplev's first suicide attempt. *Summerfolk* includes a troupe of actors who are preparing to present an entertainment, which recalls the staging of a play in the first act of *The Seagull*./5/ Yet in Gorky these elements often seem peripheral to the main action. The acting troupe never comes to play an integral role in *Summerfolk*, while Chekhov makes the play and its aftermath crucial to his work. Riumin's self-inflicted wound becomes little more than a diversion in Gorky's plot, while Treplev's eventual suicide, of course, ends *The Seagull*. Moreover, Kaleria and Shalimov never interact in the way that the rivalry between Trigorin and Treplev becomes central to Chekhov.

The loose ends evident in this play are only symptomatic of a wider problem. While their individual characters are nearly always well-sketched, in many of Gorky's early plays a plethora of both characters and intrigues hinders the emergence of central figures. Thus Leonid Andreev, in a basically positive review of *The Petty Bourgeois*, noted that all the characters in the play are primary, there being virtually no secondary roles. As a result, he said, the action passes by in confused haste and it is difficult to see exactly which characters are meant to convey Gorky's chief concerns. Actually, in that play Gorky intended Nil, the foster son of the man who heads the main family described in the work, as his protagonist./6/ Chekhov, again a discerning critic of Gorky's dramatic technique, noted that the character's part was too small; he was being asked to convey too much of the play's message without being given a chance to emerge as its chief figure./7/ That message - an attack on bourgeois society and its values - is combined with an attempt to portray the psychological complexities of the characters. In this regard, too, Gorky adds a greater burden than the play can bear. Here, as in *Summerfolk* and other early plays, he has too many things going on. In *The Lower Depths*, despite the chaos, a central figure and theme do emerge, while the "intrigue" recedes into the background. In the other plays, though, the hierarchy among characters is often not clearly established and the complexities of the plot lines tend to obscure rather than to enhance the message.

Still, even among Gorky's first plays it is possible to discern at least some hints of the features that were to distinguish his dramatic works of the 1910s. *Children of the Sun* (1905), for example, in comparison with other plays of the early period, has far fewer characters, allowing

GORKY THE DRAMATIST

each to stand out in much greater detail. On the whole, the play is a strange work and stands somewhat apart from the rest of the canon. It began as a joint project with Leonid Andreev and had the working title of *The Astronomer*. Andreev went on to write *To the Stars* (1905), while Gorky returned to the play when he was under arrest for his proclamations following the events of "Bloody Sunday", January 9, 1905./8/ The unrest of that year, combined with his original conception, produced a play about a chemist, Pavel Protasov, who is totally isolated from the life around him. When a cholera epidemic breaks out in the town, the populace suspect that the "doctors" are at fault, and so all those with even the vaguest connections with the medical profession find themselves in danger. A veterinarian hangs himself during the disturbances and Protasov's house is besieged, though the threat to him is ultimately deflected. If Gorky's choice of a scientist as his main character results from the failed collaboration with Andreev, then the theme of fear among the upper classes when faced with mass violence from below no doubt stems from the immediate influence of the events of "Bloody Sunday". Whether the resulting hybrid work forced Gorky to narrow his usually broad cast of characters or whether he simply made a conscious effort to probe a handful of figures more deeply, the result is a play in which each individual is memorable.

Nonetheless it would be wrong to claim that *Children of the Sun* represents a major breakthrough in Gorky's dramatic career. On the one hand he creates a complex central figure, a scientist who combines exalted dreams of a better future with an almost comic blindness when faced with anything that relates to everyday life./9/ On the other, both Protasov's sincere desire for a better future and his helplessness amid the ordinary world are too extreme; in the final analysis Gorky has difficulty in conveying Protasov's passion for science in a credible manner, so that the entire character is less effective than he might be. Gorky succeeds somewhat better with Vagin, an artist who has a budding affair with Protasov's wife, Elena. Vagin, like both Protasov and Elena, lacks any real understanding of ordinary people; his art has estranged him from life, just as Protasov's chemistry has cut him off from reality. However, his expressions of belief are less high-flown and his actions less clown-like than those of Protasov. If neither character is a totally successful creation, both are interesting in that Gorky at least avoids simple condemnation. Instead, he goes out of his way to stress the talent and productivity of both; their common failure is their inability to find a link between their intellectual pursuits and the rest of life around them.

The play's major failing, though, is not so much that Gorky did not create profound characters, but that he kept them too much in the background. Chepurnoy, the veterinarian who commits suicide, combines the knowledge of a Protasov or Vagin with a much greater awareness of the world at large. His profession itself is indicative: it is too practical for aesthetes, yet at the same time it requires both learning and intelligence. In his sincerity and earnestness, as well as in the way he appears to view life from an objective and at times ironic distance, Chepurnoy could well be a figure in a Chekhov play. His suicide, however, seems only weakly motivated; had Gorky developed him further, he could have emerged as one of his outstanding creations for the stage. The same is true of Protasov's sister, Liza. If Protasov seems inured to the events around him, Liza possesses a morbid fascination with and fear of violence. She is

GORKY THE DRAMATIST

in love with Chepurnoy and needs his calming influence so as not to become overwhelmed by her fears. When she witnesses the attack on her home and hears about Chepurnoy's death, the double blow unhinges her mind. While it is easier to grasp her personality than that of Chepurnoy, the play would have been improved had she too been given a larger role. As it stands, the characters in the foreground lack psychological depth, while those who possess it are only on the periphery of the main action.

A similar problem prevents *Enemies* (1906) from becoming quite as satisfactory a play as it might have been. While it has more major characters than *Children of the Sun*, it has a relatively straightforward plot. Moreover, intrigue does not overwhelm characterisation, in contrast to *Summerfolk* or *The Petty Bourgeois*. The play, like Gorky's novel *Mother* (1906), was written during his stay in the United States, and deals with the topic of revolution. A struggle between factory owners and workers is described largely from the standpoint of the owners, who are nonetheless depicted unflatteringly. The main character is Zakhar Bardin, who fulfils Gorky's concept of the typical "liberal" - a person who has good intentions but is essentially weak. He would prefer to avoid a confrontation with his workers, but when his partner is killed by an employee after declaring a lockout, Bardin lets the official investigation take its course. If the play is reasonably effective as political drama, many of its characters, all too typically for such works, resemble clichés. Zakhar is the ineffectual moderate, his partner and then the partner's widow are the cruel masters, and the niece of Zakhar's wife is the innocent young girl who becomes attracted to the workers' cause, while the workers themselves are idealistic and self-sacrificing figures.

BARRY P.SCHERR

As the American critic John Simon has noted, the "most dramatically viable characters" here are Zakhar's brother, Iakov, and Tatiana, the latter's wife./10/ These two occupy the play's limited middle ground. Tatiana, a former actress, sympathises strongly with the workers. She flirts with the brother of the dead partner in an attempt to convince him to release a worker who has been arrested in connection with the killing, but her efforts fail. At the end she seems about to join the niece of Zakhar's wife and to begin working for the revolutionaries' cause. Unlike the other people in the play, she undergoes a change. Her husband, by contrast, comes to realise that he is unable to change. He classifies himself among the loafers and tramps, the "spongers". He is a hanger-on whose sympathies lie largely with the workers but who realises that he lacks the will or energy to help them or indeed to do any good in the world at all. When he leaves Tatiana at the end of the play, he is going off to shoot himself. Both characters are sufficiently profound to serve as focal points for the play, yet their time on stage is limited. Both here and in *Children of the Sun* Gorky creates figures who are of great intrinsic interest, but because his main attention is drawn to a social issue that is best expressed through other people, he leaves his strongest creations in the shadows.

Gorky's new technique begins to emerge with his play *The Eccentrics* (1910). Superficially, it resembles such works as *Summerfolk*. The setting is once more a *dacha*, the intrigue involves a love triangle and several subsidiary triangles as well, and the characters are again educated members of Russia's bourgeois society. However, *The Eccentrics* has far fewer characters than *Summerfolk* and it relegates social issues to the back-

48

GORKY THE DRAMATIST

ground./11/   The main figure, Mastakov, is a writer who strives to convey to his readers an image of something that is good and beautiful. In many ways he recalls Protasov, the chemist in *Children of the Sun* — both are dedicated to their work, express a love of high ideals, and yet are hopeless in dealing with the people closest to them.   However, Gorky is much more convincing in depicting the writer than he was in portraying the scientist. Mastakov's naiveté is at times comic, yet he remains a credible figure, all too human in his foibles. On the one hand he is sincere in his efforts to inspire people towards a better life, but on the other his inability to resist being attracted to any woman he meets nearly destroys his marriage.   Towards the end of the play he even begins to flirt with a young woman whose fiancé has just died; though he dimly realises that the moment is absurdly inopportune, he cannot stop himself. In the end his marriage survives, but the intention of the play is to illustrate how a person can be enormously creative and yet at the same time lead a life that is far from exemplary. In *Children of the Sun* Protasov's foibles merely served as comic relief; here the clash between an individual's talents and his human frailties serves as the impetus for an entire play.

Even though the play includes one or two passing references to political issues such as the events of 1905 and the reaction to them on the part of intellectuals, the social and ideological concerns that were previously at the forefront have greatly receded. Instead, Gorky for once places the individual who is of greater interest in the spotlight, and he carefully supplements the depiction of Mastakov by surrounding him with characters who help bring out certain of his qualities. Thus his wife Elena at first seems helpless before the attempts of another woman to lure her husband away, but she turns out to appreciate the value of what he has written and to understand his weaknesses more clearly than her rival, whom she eventually defeats. Vasia, the young fiancé who dies in the course of the play, is initially admired by others for his courage when faced with death. However, he later turns out to be querulous and bitter - the process of dying brings out the worst in him, rather than the best. By contrast, Mastakov's relentlessly optimistic outlook emerges in an even more favourable light. The play's love intrigue and its social setting are secondary; all is subordinated to illustrating aspects of the main figure's personality.

Another less positive, but no less compelling strong central figure distinguishes Gorky's other main dramatic work of 1910, *Vassa Zheleznova*. As Zakhar Zheleznov, a successful merchant, lies dying offstage during the play's first two acts, his wife Vassa joins battle with her sons and Zakhar's brother for the inheritance. Although the law is largely on the side of her sons, she uses great cunning to gain control over the money and to rout her own children. If that were all that the play involved, though, it would simply be a study in evil, but Vassa is a much more complex figure./12/ The play has the subtitle *Mother*, which, despite Vassa's cunning and greed, is not meant altogether ironically. She is in fact protective towards those whom she loves - one of her daughters-in-law, and also her own daughter. Furthermore, her desire to gain control over her husband's business stems from a genuine wish to prevent her incompetent sons from destroying what she and her husband have built up over the years The struggles that she has had to endure have taken their toll on her: at the end of the play she mentions that she hears voices and feels that she

GORKY THE DRAMATIST

will never know any peace. The contradictory qualities of Vassa would make her into a tragic figure if the good outweighed the evil. In the final analysis she bears the guilt for too many wrongs, yet she had at least some good motives, and by the end is all too aware of the burden of her crimes.

As in *The Eccentrics*, the surface appearance of a character can be deceptive. Vasia seemed courageous, but was in fact fearful of death; Elena at first acted as though she were helpless to combat Mastakov's vagaries, but turned out to be much stronger than her rivals. Here Vassa begins as an embodiment of wickedness, plotting against her own children and possibly encouraging others to hasten her husband's death; at the end, though, she has been transformed into an almost benevolent tyrant for whom power entails punishment as well as reward.

Over the next few years Gorky was to pursue the path that he embarked on in these two plays. He wrote works that have only a handful of characters and generally only one or two plot lines, instead of the massive casts and involved intrigues of the early plays. Formerly, his main characters were generally negative, while the more positive figures played secondary roles. But already in the plays of 1910 a change has taken place. Vassa is hardly everyone's idea of a kindly mother, but what makes her into a powerful figure on stage is the presence of good qualities that at least partly offset the bad. And Mastakov, for all his failings, is ultimately an attractive figure, gaining by the close at least a measure of self-awareness - in contrast to his predecessor, Protasov, who remained blind to his own failings to the very end. Interestingly, after 1910 Gorky's positive characters tend to be not workers or representatives of the lower classes, but more frequently merchants. The few members of that class who do appear in the earlier plays are hardly likeable, but it should be remembered that strong merchant figures are by no means rare in Gorky's novels. There, too, both weaker and more negative figures tend to stand to the fore, but in more than one instance - for example, in *Foma Gordeev* (1899) and *The Artamonov Business* (1925) - the founder of a family enterprise, while not totally admirable, nonetheless possesses redeeming qualities. What is unusual in Gorky's late plays is his decision to make such merchants his main figures and to treat them, despite their glaring faults, quite sympathetically. Finally, even though social concerns continue to play a role in *Vassa Zheleznova* - her class, if not Vassa herself, stands condemned - Gorky increasingly turns away from ideology and moves towards broader philosophical and psychological issues. Of particular note is his continuing dialogue, perhaps better termed a polemic, with Dostoevsky - a writer whom Gorky admired for his talent but detested for his ideas./13/

Dostoevsky was very much on Gorky's mind when he wrote *The Zykovs* (1914). He was sufficiently incensed by the decision of the Moscow Art Theatre to stage works based on Dostoevsky's *The Brothers Karamazov* and *The Possessed* that he published a harshly critical article on "Karamazovism" and placed such restrictive conditions on an earlier agreement allowing the Theatre to stage his next play, that the co-director, Nemirovich-Danchenko, eventually refused *The Zykovs*./14/ Gorky now challenges the Dostoevskian notion that spiritual goodness is associated with meekness./15/ Antipa Zykov, a timber merchant, brushes his weak and indecisive son aside to marry Pavla, a girl who has lived for several years in a convent. Pavla is meek, but she manages to disrupt the lives of those around her. A forester who had once killed a man but was freed through Antipa's efforts, becomes so unnerved by Pavla's pitying looks that he resolves to seek work elsewhere. Pavla herself resumes her courtship with Antipa's son, Mikhail, while Antipa himself is driven to distraction by her. For all her apparent passivity and innocence, Pavla only sows discord and so has a devastating effect on the family.

Sofia, Antipa's sister, is a more positive version of Vassa. She, too, assumes the burden of power and sacrifices her own well-being. Having married a dying man at her brother's request, she spends her widowhood helping in the business. She turns aside efforts to court her so as to place her brother and the welfare of the business above personal happiness Her dedication and determination are qualities that Gorky clearly admires; indeed, it is her resolve that helps reunite father and son. At the end Pavla is asked to leave, and a more harmonious future for the family seems assured.

Towards the end of Act II Sofia continues the implicit polemic with Dostoevsky:

> Sofia: I'd like to sin, to raise a ruckus, break all the laws, mess up everything. And then, once I'd risen above the people, I'd throw myself at their feet. "Dear people, my own people! I'm not your master, but a lowly sinner, lower than anyone; you don't have any masters, you don't need them..."
> Pavla (softly, in a frightened voice): Why do that? What do you want?
> Sofia: To free people from fear of each other...there's no need to be afraid of anyone! But everyone is frightened and repressed, they live in fear./16/

The first part of Sofia's speech may appear to be more pro- than anti-Dostoevsky, but her final point clearly differs: while wanting people to liberate themselves, she also advocates strength and pride in the self. In

BARRY P.SCHERR

Gorky's view meekness becomes the source of evil, while goodness flows from those who, like Sofia, have power and use it well.

Antipa, the play's ostensible hero, both attracts and repels. His physical stamina and love of work enable him to build a successful business from which many benefit, but he also deals ruthlessly with those around him and does not even stop at crushing his own son. Here, too, Gorky comes down on the side of strength: Antipa at one point excuses his treatment of his son by citing the latter's weakness, while both Sofia and Antipa are given speeches in which they see themselves as two struggling individuals whose wealth and success justify their lives. So it is that in *The Zykovs* Gorky manages to create not one but several central characters who are presented in sharp relief. Their interactions are carefully designed to illustrate not only their inner contradictions but also the play's main thematic concerns. With its finely-wrought dramatic conflicts, this must be considered one of Gorky's most satisfying works for the stage.

The most unusual of Gorky's plays is *The Counterfeit Coin* (1913/1927), a work that still awaits an English rendition. The play deals with another question that is important to Dostoevsky - that of suffering and its potentially purifying effects - but the main influence in this case would appear to be not Dostoevsky but a writer whose name is rarely associated with Gorky, Pirandello./17/ The play's main characters are Polina, wife of the watchmaker Iakovlev, and Stogov, a person who wronged her several years previously. Stogov arrives at the house where Iakovlev has his shop and expresses an interest in counterfeiters. He renews his acquaintance with Polina, but then becomes diverted by her step-daughter, Natasha. Iakovlev is by nature cruel; his loss of an eye is the physical reflection

GORKY THE DRAMATIST

of his moral deficiency.   (He is apparently based on a suitor of Gorky's mother who is described briefly in *Childhood*, on which Gorky was working at the time he wrote the original version of this play).   Polina has suffered as Iakovlev's wife, just as earlier she suffered because of her relationship with Stogov.   When Stogov abandons her again, the added suffering leads not to her purification but to her suicide. The final version of the play, which was completed only in the mid-1920s, differs significantly, especially in its final act, from the original draft of 1913. In the first version the character who was to become Stogov was clearly a counterfeiter himself; affected by Polina's inner goodness, he was about to embark on a new and happy life with her at the end of the play.

While the original concept of the play may well owe something to Pirandello's stories, Gorky's reworking of it creates similarities with Pirandello's major works of the 1920s, and most notably with his *Six Characters in Search of an Author* (1921).   Both the first and second versions of *The Counterfeit Coin* were written when Gorky was living in Italy, and he was no doubt familiar with Pirandello's work.   As in Pirandello, but uniquely among Gorky's dramatic writings, *The Counterfeit Coin* deals at length with the question of illusion and reality, of what is false and what is real. The entire play is cloaked in mystery. When writing to the German translator of the play, Gorky stated outright that Stogov was a detective who had appeared in the town in order to catch counterfeiters./18/ Within the play itself, however, it is hard to be sure. Even though at one point Stogov tells Natasha that he is a detective, he himself earlier tried to lure Iakovlev into a counterfeiting scheme. Other identities are also unclear. Natasha turns out to be the daughter not of Iakovlev, but of

BARRY P. SCHERR

Kemskoi, the owner of the house in which they live. Polina's past appears only in fragments and is never fully elucidated. The mad Luzgin, who has ostensibly come to have a watch repaired, ends up unsure of his or anybody else's identity. As it turns out, Stogov is no more able than Luzgin to determine identities and to find out who the real counterfeiters are. He has a similar difficulty with coins: to distinguish a false coin from the real, he has to mark it with a needle. He then tells Natasha that you can distinguish a real person from a false one only by placing a mark on him, but then that person is spoiled. In this play Gorky gives his characters depth in a way that is new for him: by hinting rather than by explaining, and by deliberately leaving gaps that the audience must attempt to fill. The result is a gripping if at times eerie work that shows a new subtlety and finesse in his depiction of human nature.

The last play that Gorky was to complete before he returned to dramatic work near the end of his career was *The Old Man* (1915). Again, he manages to get by here with only a handful of characters and a comparatively simple plot. The hero, Mastakov, is a more likeable version of Antipa Zykov; he has managed to do much in the town even though he is surrounded by people far less skilled and less energetic than himself. However, the "old man", Pitirim, wanders back into his life. It turns out that Mastakov has hidden from all the fact that he was once sent to prison for a murder that he did not commit. After escaping, he began life anew in the town. Pitirim was a fellow-prisoner who has served his term and now travels about as a tramp, accompanied by a young woman who was herself imprisoned after the death of her baby.

Perhaps more than any of Gorky's plays, *The Old Man* shows an affinity

GORKY THE DRAMATIST

with one of his great predecessors in European drama, Henrik Ibsen. Along with Chekhov and Gorky, Ibsen was one of the playwrights whose works were frequently staged by the Moscow Art Theatre. Indeed, in the early years of the twentieth century, just as Gorky was developing as a dramatist, Ibsen's works were regularly appearing with his as part of that Theatre's seasonal repertoire./19/ Moreover, Gorky's letters show that he knew and valued Ibsen's works, and it is easy to cite similarities in their thematic concerns, particularly between Ibsen's earlier, more socially-oriented plays, and Gorky's works. The question of direct influence, though, is more difficult to resolve, but certainly many of Gorky's characters, even if treated differently within his plays, seem to owe their origin at least partly to Ibsen. Perhaps it is sufficient to cite the resemblance between Vassa Zheleznova and John Gabriel Borkman (in the play of that name), whose past showed a similar mixture of power and ambition, and the toll that both can take on the individual.

However, the thematic concerns of Ibsen's late plays and his extremely spare, concentrated manner are in direct contrast to most of Gorky's work. It is only in certain plays of the 1910s - *The Counterfeit Coin* and particularly *The Old Man* - that a more profound similarity between Gorky and Ibsen is to be found. For one thing, the atmosphere of these late plays recalls that of Ibsen, for whom "reality is a vision of consciousness and is undeniably pessimistic. The oppressions and restrictions are intrinsic and irredeemable. The final focus ... is upon a dissolving sense of reality"./20/ Gorky's universe, at least in these last two plays, is equally dark. Occasionally, specific thematic parallels arise too - thus in *The Wild Duck* (1884) Gregers Werle's obsession with exposing the truth leads to another's suicide, much as does Stogov's attempt in *The Counterfeit Coin* to determine what is real. In both cases a professedly idealistic outsider becomes the bearer of death. Ibsen often favoured a peculiar dramatic structure, in which much of the key action has taken place *before* the play opens (*John Gabriel Borkman* [1896] and *Rosmersholm* [1886] are but two examples); the same device appears in both *The Counterfeit Coin* and *The Old Man*./21/ Perhaps most crucial, though, is the smaller cast that Gorky comes to employ. Like Ibsen, he learns to concentrate on a handful of main characters. While *The Old Man* has eleven characters, only four of them are of any real importance, and the conflict ultimately boils down to just two: Mastakov and Pitirim. By creating dramatic tension largely out of events that have occurred before the play begins and by probing the psyches of his protagonists more deeply than before, Gorky creates a powerful narrative, which may well have resulted from the belated but beneficial influence of Ibsen on his dramatic technique.

In a preface written for the first English translation of *The Old Man* (which was entitled *The Judge*), Gorky stated his theme directly: "In *The Judge* ... I have tried to show how repulsive a man may be who becomes infatuated with his own suffering, who has come to believe that he enjoys the right to torment others for what he has suffered"./22/ Thus Pitirim seeks retribution from Mastakov, who did not serve out his full prison term and who neither in jail nor afterwards has suffered as he did. If he simply wanted money, Mastakov could probably have satisfied him, but the monetary reward Pitirim seeks is only of secondary importance. He wants Mastakov to suffer out of a desire for vengeance, and to make him do so, he keeps him off balance by never revealing just what would satisfy

GORKY THE DRAMATIST

him - indeed, Pitirim himself seems more interested in suffering for its own sake than in any goal that he can define. Caught in a trap from which he cannot free himself, Mastakov escapes in the only way he knows - through suicide.

Thematically the play contains Gorky's most direct attack on Dostoevsky's depiction of suffering. Dostoevsky, of course, felt that some higher goal was important; in a number of works he specifically rejected suffering for its own sake. However, Gorky feels that no higher good can ever result from voluntarily accepting suffering, no matter what the purpose. In the three final plays of this period he is also denying the right of any individual to pass judgment on another. Pavla's judgments lead to discord and despair, Stogov comes to realise that he cannot tell the false from the real, and Pitirim's verdict only destroys a good person and forces Pitirim himself to leave the town empty-handed.

A further development among the three plays can be seen in Gorky's treatment of suicide. Plays in general seem to contain a relatively greater number of suicides than other literary works do, perhaps because suicide serves as an effective device for culminating a psychological crisis that needs to be portrayed on stage over the course of just two or three hours. Among Gorky's predecessors, suicide occurs in the works of Chekhov (*The Seagull*), but it is especially common in Ibsen: note *The Wild Duck*, *Hedda Gabler* (1890), and, especially, *Rosmersholm*, which ends with a double suicide. Suicide or attempted suicide is a motif in Gorky's early plays as well, but now he is careful to introduce it precisely at the moment of greatest dramatic tension. In *The Zykovs* the son, Mikhail, shoots himself at the end of the penultimate act, the third, after an altercation with his father over Pavla. His wound is not serious (Gorky's weaker characters tend to have difficulty even in harming themselves), but the shock of the attempt leads to a reconciliation with his father and to the expulsion of Pavla from the household. Polina's suicide is announced at the very end of *The Counterfeit Coin*, just as the other characters are attempting to subdue the crazed Luzgin. Her death is the logical outcome of her bitter disappointment, and it bears witness to the crueller side of Stogov's apparent search for justice. It is necessary only to compare these two episodes with moments in earlier plays by Gorky to see the progression in his dramatic technique. Riumin's attempted suicide in *Summerfolk* was no more than an aside to the plot, while the Actor's death, announced at the very end of *The Lower Depths* in a manner not all that different from that seen in *The Counterfeit Coin*, is dramatically effctive but not well-motivated psychologically./23/ Only in *The Old Man*, though, does Gorky have the most important character in the entire play commit suicide. In the final analysis this work is not simply about retribution, (which would make Pitirim its most important character), but also about human frailty, about how a decent person can become enmeshed in an intrigue from which death would seem to provide the only release.

In their creation of striking and complex central figures, in their concern with moral questions of universal significance, and in their spare but intensely dramatic structure, the plays that Gorky wrote during the years immediately after 1910, and especially the last three works of the period, constitute major achievements in his career as a playwright. While none of these works has captured the popular imagination in the way that *The Lower Depths* has, all are deserving of more attention than they have

GORKY THE DRAMATIST

received. Indeed, as has been argued here, in their mastery they may well surpass the plays for which Gorky has been better known by generations of audiences./24/

NOTES

1. A.P.Chekhov, *Polnoe sobranie sochinenii i pisem v tridtsati tomakh: pis'ma v dvenadtsati tomakh* (Moscow, 1974-83), Vol.11, p.12.
2. See L.M.Farber, "Kompozitsionnoe svoeobrazie *Na dne* M.Gor'kogo", in *Gor'kovskie chteniia 1976: materialy konferentsii "A.M.Gor'kogo i teatr"*, ed. I.K.Kuz'michev (Gorky, 1977), pp.87-90.
3. See V.L.L'vov-Rogachevskii, "Maksim Gor'kii", in *Russkaia literatura XX veka (1890-1910)*, ed. S.A.Vengerov (Moscow, 1914), Vol.1, p.211.
4. See Iu.Iuzovskii, *"Na dne" M.Gor'kogo: idei i obrazy* (Moscow, 1968), pp.126-37.
5. See Harold B.Segel, *Twentieth-Century Russian Drama: From Gorky to the Present* (New York, 1979), pp.15-16.
6. In a letter to Stanislavsky, Gorky characterised Nil as "a person calmly confident of his own strength and of his right to remake life and all of its systems according to his understanding. And his understanding flows from a healthy, spirited feeling of love for life". (M. Gor'kii, *Sobranie sochinenii v tridtsati tomakh* (Moscow, 1949-56), Vol. 28, p.219.
7. Chekhov, *Pis'ma*, Vol.2, pp.95-6.
8. For an account of this play's complicated "pre-history", see S.D.Balukhatyi, "Rabota M.Gor'kogo nad p'esoi *Deti solntsa* (Materialy i nabliudeniia)", in *M.Gor'kii: materialy i issledovaniia*, ed. V.A.Desnitskii (Leningrad, 1934), Vol.1, pp.459-62.
9. On the contradictions in Protasov's depiction, see B.A.Bialik, *M. Gor'kii - dramaturg* (Moscow, 1962), p.247.
10. John Simon, *Uneasy Stages: A Chronicle of the New York Theater, 1963-1973* (New York, 1975), pp.432-3.
11. For a detailed comparison of this play with *Summerfolk*, see S.V.Kastorskii, *Dramaturgiia M.Gor'kogo: nabliudeniia nad ideino-khudozhestvennoi spetsifikoi* (Moscow-Leningrad, 1963), pp.92-5.
12. Soviet critics have often indicated a preference for the less complex and more clearly negative figure of Vassa that appears in the drastically revised version of the play which Gorky prepared in the 1930s. See, for example, I.A.Bocharova, "Dve Vassy", in *Gor'kovskie chteniia 1959-1960* (Moscow, 1962), Vol.7, p.181.
13. For an account of Gorky's literary and critical commentaries on Dostoevsky, see B.A.Bialik, "Dostoevskii i dostoevshchina v otsenkakh Gor'kogo", in *Tvorchestvo Dostoevskogo*, ed. N.L.Stepanov (Moscow, 1959), pp. 65-100.
14. These conditions were laid down in a letter from Gorky to the publisher Ivan Ladyzhnikov. See *Arkhiv A.M.Gor'kogo* (Moscow, 1959), Vol.7, p.227.

15. On this play's treatment of Dostoevskian themes, see Bialik, *M.Gor'kii - dramaturg*, pp.300-09.
16. M.Gor'kii, *Polnoe sobranie sochinenii: khudozhestvennye proizvedeniia v dvadtsati piati tomakh* (Moscow, 1968-76), Vol.13, p.326.
17. See A.A.Volkov, *Put' khudozhnika: M.Gor'kii do Oktiabria* (Moscow, 1969), pp.310-13.
18. The full text of Gorky's remarks about his play can be found in *PSS*: XIII,535-7.
19. For a detailed discussion of similarities (as well as differences) between Gorky's plays and Ibsen's, see the article by B.V.Mikhailovskii, "Gor'kii i Ibsen", in his *Izbrannye stat'i po literature i isskustve* (Moscow, 1969), pp.247-91. The Moscow Art Theatre's presentations of Ibsen's works are detailed on pp.250-3.
20. Charles R.Lyons, *Henrik Ibsen: The Divided Consciousness* (Carbondale, Ill., 1972), p.167.
21. See Mikhailovskii, *op. cit.*, p.287.
22. Maxim Gorky, *The Judge: A Play in Four Acts*, tr. Marie Zakrevsky and Barrett H.Clark (New York, 1924), pp.vii-viii.
23. Chekhov wrote to Gorky that "the death of the actor is terrible. You hit the spectator over the head with this for no apparent reason, without having prepared for it". (*Pis'ma*, Vol.11, p.12).
24. An earlier version of this paper was read at the March, 1986 meeting of the New England Slavic Association in Boston, U.S.A. I would like to thank Edith Clowes, Betty Forman and Melissa Smith for several suggestions that I have since incorporated into my article.

* * * * *

VSEVOLOD GARSHIN AND THE EARLY GORKY:

SOME ARTISTIC AND CULTURAL LINKS AND AFFINITIES

Peter Henry

University of Glasgow,

Scotland

This article deals with two interrelated issues in Gorky's literary ancestry and his early stories that would appear to require further investigation. They are: (1) his links and affinities with the writer Vsevolod Garshin (1855-88), which have not yet been systematically dealt with, and (2) his early short story *A Mistake*, which has not received the critical attention it deserves./1/ An attempt is made here to fill these gaps and, thirdly, to relate *A Mistake* to Garshin's short story *The Red Flower*, a comparison that seems not only overdue but also highly appropriate. The two works are reviewed here not so much as biographical "evidence" - something done by several scholars in both East and West - but as pieces of (realist? impressionist? modernist?) fiction. The emphasis is on the writers' treatment of mental illness and on the way they developed the romantic concept of insanity, a concept whereby the madman, endowed with a superior awareness, is both the new hero, the man of the future "in disguise", and, though rejected by society, a "genius" who formulates a heroic vision of the future.

I

When in 1898 Gorky's early stories first appeared in book form, N.K.

PETER HENRY

Mikhailovsky, editor of the Populist monthly *Russkoe bogatstvo*, published two major review articles in his journal./2/ In the second he wrote at length on *A Mistake*,/3/ rightly describing it as "a strange story that stands on its own in Mr. Gorky's two slim volumes"./4/ It is, indeed, "a strange story" and was, moreover, a red rag to the magisterial spokesman for the Populist view on literary and ideological matters. Mikhailovsky saw it as "demonstrating the dangers that threaten the author on his subsequent literary path"./5/ Disturbed by the symptoms of "decadence" that he discerned in the story, the critic singled out a character's remark that "the decadents are subtle people. Fine as needles, they pierce deeply into the unknown" (I,104), and launched into a diatribe against "decadence". Mikhailovsky, who must have known that in 1896 Gorky had published his own attack on decadence - "Paul Verlaine and the Decadents"/6/ - sensed, on good grounds, that the young author was attracted to the new trend. Mikhailovsky concluded by turning the utterance round: "...the fine sharp needles of decadence are in fact neither fine nor sharp, but, on the contrary, very coarse and blunt";/7/ rather than achieving ideal clarity, the decadent approach produces a "fog" of vagueness and uncertainty. The fact that the offending remark had been made by a fictional madman did not, in Mikhailovsky's view, invalidate his diagnosis that the author too was afflicted by the dread disease. The other "danger" - and it was a major one allegedly threatening the young Gorky - was the influence of Nietzsche, *nichsheanstvo* (Mikhailovsky's spelling), manifested in *A Mistake* and other early stories.

A Mistake certainly "stands on its own" in the 1898 collection. It does not deal with tramps and other outcasts whom Gorky met in his wanderings

GARSHIN AND THE EARLY GORKY

through Russia in the famine years of 1891 and 1892 and earlier; nor does it relate an exotic legend drawn from Russian, Tartar or Caucasian folklore.

The history of the composition and publication of *A Mistake* is briefly as follows. Its conception dates from Gorky's sojourn in Tiflis in 1891-2, but the story was only written up three years later, in Nizhny-Novgorod, in 1894. Early in 1895 Gorky submitted it, via Korolenko, to *Russkoe bogatstvo*, but it was rejected by Mikhailovsky. Later that year it appeared in *Russkaia mysl'*, again through Korolenko's mediation, and was included in the 1898 edition of Gorky's stories.

From Odessa, where he had worked as a stevedore, Gorky went on in 1891 to Simferopol, Yalta, Feodosia, Kerch, Taman and the Kuban, arriving in Tiflis on 1st November of that year. There he met the prototype of the story's main character.

Gorky's stay in Tiflis has been fully documented, and its crucial importance for his personal and ideological development - above all, for his emergence as a writer - has been amply attested by numerous contemporaries/8/ and by Gorky himself./9/ Of major importance were his activities in the local "commune", to which an oblique reference is made in *A Mistake*. He met numerous Russian political exiles, including former members of The People's Will, and several Georgian pre-Marxist socialists and revolutionaries.

Initially, Gorky shared M.Ia.Nachalov's room - both had been members of the Nizhny-Novgorod "circle" - and Nachalov not only found him work in the Trans-Caucasian Railway offices but also introduced him to other political exiles. Later Gorky lodged with Ia.A.Danko, whom he had also met previous-

65

ly, in Perm. Danko had worked in the Perm locomotive repair sheds as a boilermaker's mate. These men were popularly known as *glukhari*, a colloquial term for "deaf men"./10/ Here we find possibly the first link between the writers: it was probably when seeing *glukhari* at work in Perm that Gorky first read Garshin's works, among them *Artists* (1879), where the gruelling work of a *glukhar'* is graphically described./11/ Gorky's several references to *Artists* indicate that the story had particularly impressed him.

In Tiflis he also met V.V.Bervi-Flerovsky, author of seminal works such as *The Condition of the Working Class in Russia* (1869) and *The Alphabet of the Social Sciences* (1871), a man whom the young Gorky rightly valued as a social thinker. So, incidentally, had the young Garshin, who read the latter work as a seventeen-year-old schoolboy soon after its publication, and wrote excitedly to his mother: "I'm reading Flerovsky's *Alphabet of the Social Sciences* – it's simply marvellous!"./12/

For Gorky's emergence as a writer the most important person he met in Tiflis was undoubtedly A.M.Kaliuzhny (1853-1939). A former member of S.F. Kovalik's "circle" in Kharkov, Kaliuzhny had been repeatedly exiled for his political activities. Gorky always remained grateful for his moral and material support at the beginning of his literary career. Writing to him from Sorrento thirty-three years later, he acknowledged that Kaliuzhny had been the first man to regard him "with genuine humaneness", and not merely as "a chap from some queer biography, an aimless tramp, something amusing but dubious". Kaliuzhny had sensed his literary potential and made the budding writer "look seriously at myself. I owe it to your incentive that for the last thirty years I have been honourably serving Russian art"./13/

GARSHIN AND THE EARLY GORKY

It was in Kaliuzhny's room (where he stayed in June-July, 1892) and under his supervision that Gorky completed his first published story, *Makar Chudra*, his host arranging its publication in the Tiflis newspaper *Kavkaz*, on 12/24 September, 1892. At this point, too, the symbolic transformation of Aleksei Maksimovich Peshkov into Maxim Gorky took place: *Makar Chudra* was published over the famous pseudonym which had occurred to the author while in the newspaper's editorial office. Although Kaliuzhny was undeniably important for him at this stage, Gorky himself contributed to an exaggerated version of Kaliuzhny's role in his life./14/ An oddly persistent legend has it that Kaliuzhny applied a form of house arrest to the writer until the story was completed./15/ Kaliuzhny, too, has left important reminiscences about the genesis of *A Mistake*./16/

One of the many politically active Georgians whom Gorky met in Tiflis was N.Ia. (Niko) Nikoladze, editor of the liberal journal *Novoe obozrenie*, a former associate of Chernyshevsky, Dobroliubov, Herzen and Nekrasov. Nikoladze had been a contributor to the Petersburg journal *Otechestvennye zapiski*, where in 1882 he had published an important article on Garshin's early stories./17/ Nikoladze dealt primarily with *Attalea Princeps* (1879), a romantic allegory on the will to liberty which he and many other contemporaries presumed to have been inspired by the fanatical heroism of The People's Will./18/ Another Georgian acquaintance, S.A. Vartaniants (Vartanov), left valuable reminiscences of Gorky in Tiflis/19/ and was one of the prototypes of Iaroslavtsev, the antagonist in *A Mistake*./20/ As regards that story, however, the most important Georgian whom Gorky met was Gola (Grigorii) Chitadze (c.1862-92), the undisputed prototype of Kravtsov, the story's main character.

As Gorky later explained, Chitadze was

> the son of a peasant, one of the first propagators of Marxism among the younger men ... in Tiflis. He was very popular in particular among the workers and was in contact with the revolutionaries of The People's Will who had been sentenced at the Trial of the Fifty. His hard work, his studies and hunger caused his mind to become afflicted with *mania grandiosa*./21/

Chitadze was admitted to an asylum where he died just three days later, his death occurring, apparently, after an orderly threw him down a staircase.

Gorky spent several days with Chitadze - he was later to claim that he spent nine consecutive days and nights with the sick man. The experience was "very frightening", as Chitadze was violent and assaulted those looking after him:

> Several times he tried to kill me... Once he almost killed his landlady, another time he threw a policeman down the stairs... Several times I had to bind him and then, with a madman's cunning, he would start weeping and complaining that it was hurting him; I would go up to him and release him - and he would spit in my face, roaring with laughter when he had hit the target./22/

Vartaniants recorded that during this, his terminal illness, Chitadze when lucid "evolved a whole theory on the salvation of people and their renewal; at such times he would be transformed ... into an inspired prophet ... we would forget that a madman was talking to us"./23/

It is hardly surprising that this strange, larger-than-life figure greatly intrigued Gorky. He was particularly impressed by Chitadze's unusual visions, expressed in esoteric and often poetic language. They were not very different from his own aspirations at this time, when he was also so impressed by the strong, exceptional and preferably exotic individual. Contemporaries recalled seeing Gorky note down Chitadze's speeches there and then, while the sick man was temporarily calm./24/ This would

GARSHIN AND THE YOUNG GORKY

account for the extraordinary vividness of the nocturnal scene in Kravtsov-Chitadze's moonlit room and of what may well be an unedited record of what Chitadze actually said. However, preserving this account virtually intact brought Gorky several ideological and structural problems when writing *A Mistake* three years later.

If the factual content of Gorky's story was mental illness closely observed, Garshin's work is based on his own experience of insanity – "it is a fantastic sort of thing, though in fact it is strictly real", as he said./25/ The victim of intermittent, hereditary insanity, Garshin suffered a major breakdown in 1880, induced partly by the mounting political crisis and more specifically by the traumatic failure of his private Utopian mission that February – he had personally interceded to save a young terrorist who had attempted to assassinate Count Loris-Melikov, the then quasi-liberal "dictator" of Russia./26/ Later that year Garshin was admitted to an asylum near Kharkov, and *The Red Flower* is also a "true" record – "apart from the end, everything ... is true. I didn't add anything invented by myself", as Garshin is on record as saying./27/

There are striking similarities between the manic states of Garshin's autobiographical hero and of Chitadze, notably their exceptional strengths and fanatical obsessions: Garshin's Patient was not only strait-jacketed but also strapped to his bed, and he displayed similar strength and cunning when he freed himself, forced his way through the barred window and scaled a high wall in order to pick "the last flower". Both characters are *bortsy ponevole* (instinctive fighters), as Nikoladze had aptly entitled his essay on Garshin's stories. And both authors knew enough about despair to attempt suicide – Gorky at the age of eighteen in 1887, Garshin several

69

times and finally in 1888, aged thirty-three.

II

Only twelve years separate the publication dates of these two stories, both of which were seen by some reviewers, inadequately, as "psychiatric sketches"./28/ Garshin's The Red Flower appeared in 1883,/29/ Gorky's A Mistake, as stated, in 1895./30/ In 1883 Garshin was at the height of his creative powers and of his considerable popularity with the reading public and The Red Flower is, along with From the Reminiscences of Private Ivanov (also published in 1883), his most significant and popular work. By contrast, in 1895 Gorky was taking "his first uncertain steps" in creative writing and had not yet published anything in a "fat" journal.

The plot of A Mistake can be summarised as follows. Kirill Ivanovich Iaroslavtsev, a statistician and unemployed rural teacher, has been asked by fellow-statisticians to help care for a colleague, Mark Danilovich Kravtsov, who has suddenly been seized by insanity, thereby endangering his own life and showing aggression towards those looking after him. His condition is diagnosed as *mania grandiosa*. Although in a precarious mental condition himself - with marked symptoms of persecution mania - Iaroslavtsev takes his turn at Kravtsov's bedside and stays with him throughout the night listening, at first sceptically, to his rambling monologues. They consist of aphoristic and fragmentary denunciations of contemporary life, where people's activities and even their thoughts are rigidly controlled by the authorities, reducing men to mental inactivity. His positive message is an ecstatic vision of the salvation and regeneration of mankind, with himself as the teacher and prophet of the new life.

GARSHIN AND THE EARLY GORKY

Iaroslavtsev is progressively infected by Kravtsov's "insane" vision and becomes his first disciple. The following morning both men are delivered to a mental hospital, where they continue their earnest discussions of the new order that they will bring in.

Several critics commented on the story when it first appeared, Gorky himself rated it important among his works, and Vladimir Pozner wrote in his *Panorama de la littérature russe contemporaine*: "Le succès de ces premières nouvelles, qui s'appellent: *Malva, Erreur, Tchelkach,* [dépassa] toutes les prévisions"./31/ However, the story's popularity has since declined and it is virtually unknown in the English-speaking world.

Garshin's much better-known story deals with an anonymous lunatic (*bol'noi*) who identifies a poppy in the hospital garden as containing all the evil of the world; he comes to see it as his ordained task to destroy the plant and so liberate the world from evil. His obsession escalates at an alarming rate as he engages in a "spectral struggle" with the cosmic enemy concealed in the flower, and he ultimately dies from exhaustion, happy in the belief that by destroying "the last poppy" he has fulfilled his historic mission.

D.S.Mirsky saw *The Red Flower* as initiating "a long row of lunatic-asylum stories", the next in line being Chekhov's *Ward Number Six*./32/ *A Mistake* certainly qualifies for inclusion in Mirsky's list; indeed, the relevance, direct or indirect, of Chekhov's story for Gorky's is very noticeable, as commentators were quick to point out./33/ Of no less importance is Chekhov's *The Black Monk*, which also deals explicitly with *mania grandiosa*, though very differently from Gorky's tale./34/ As regards the obvious affinities between *A Mistake* and the two Chekhov stories, one

PETER HENRY

notes that the genesis of *A Mistake* dates from 1891-2, and that *Ward Number Six* was published in 1892; *The Black Monk* appeared early in 1894, the year when Gorky was writing *A Mistake*.

Affinities with Garshin's story were instantly noted by Korolenko, who said that Gorky's work "reminds one of Garshin's *Scarlet Flower* [sic: *Alyi tsvetok*], where this form of mood [i.e. manic obsession] stands out with arresting clarity and power"./35/ The Soviet scholar B.V.Mikhailovsky rightly points out, à *propos* of Korolenko's comment, that juxtaposing these stories requires the critic to do rather more than merely offer a psychological comparison./36/ Another Soviet scholar, V.Ia.Grechnev, also acknowledged affinities between the two works when he wrote that during the 1890s "Gorky produced ... psychological sketches in some way reminiscent of Garshin's works (*A Mistake*)"./37/ Regrettably, neither Korolenko nor the Soviet scholars expanded on what they meant by this alleged similarity. I.A.Gruzdev's comment on the two stories will be discussed below.

Gorky's own scattered comments on Garshin and his works are not nearly as comprehensive as what he said and wrote about Saltykov-Shchedrin, Pomialovsky, Leskov, Uspensky, Korolenko, Karonin-Petropavlovsky and other "democratic" writers of whose literary and social activities he approved and whose lead he followed. Nevertheless, he acknowledged his affection and respect for Garshin the man and stressed the importance of his personality, attitudes and writings both for the 1880s and subsequent generations. At various times in his literary career he used his considerable influence to assure Garshin's rightful, if relatively minor, place in the pantheon of Russian writers. Indeed, Garshin's enduring popularity, the fact that his works are printed in large annual editions and are included

GARSHIN AND THE EARLY GORKY

in the syllabus of secondary schools, let alone the healthy state of Soviet Garshin studies - none of this, given his limited output and certain ideological vagaries, would probably have come about without Gorky's blessing, tacit or otherwise. However, Gorky's support is, of course, only one of the reasons for Garshin's solid standing in the Soviet Union.

In 1912 Gorky praised Ovsianiko-Kulikovsky for including an article on Garshin in his *History of Russian Literature*;/38/ his insistence, eighteen years later, that Academiia include the complete works of Garshin in its publishing programme is in the same key./39/ He singled out Garshin, "that fine and sensitive writer", as having made the outstanding Russian contribution (in *The Legend of Haggai the Proud*, 1886) to "that difficult literary form, the allegory"./40/ In 1912, when asked by a German publisher what works should be included in a projected series of Russian novellas in German translation, Gorky recommended *Four Days* (1877) and *From the Reminiscences of Private Ivanov*, Garshin's two best, though artistically very disparate war stories, based on his experiences in the Russo-Turkish War of 1877-8./41/ (Did Gorky choose the title for his story *Three Days* (1912) entirely without the influence, conscious or otherwise, of Garshin's famous *Four Days*?) In a letter to his wife in 1909 he contrasted Garshin's, Uspensky's and Korolenko's social and personal stance favourably with that of "new" writers like Kuprin./42/ He recorded a conversation with Karonin-Petropavlovsky who saw Garshin as representing the messianic element in Russian literature./43/ The revolutionary poet P.F.Iakubovich sought to persuade Gorky to revise his sceptical attitude towards the Petersburg pleiad of writers of the recent past; writing in 1900, Iakubovich, author of one of the first important articles on

Garshin,/44/ had reminded Gorky that "here were ... Saltykov, Uspensky, Shelgunov, Novodvorsky, Garshin, Nadson and many other men, their souls as pure as crystal and bright like the stars of the heavens"./45/ Thirty years on, Gorky told Soviet writers that in their work "there is no characteristic language, none of that which makes it easy to distinguish Leskov from Garshin, Garshin from Bunin"./46/

On the critical side, Gorky bracketed Garshin with Nekrasov, Dostoevsky Tolstoy and Kuprin in his vigorous and wittily-worded critique of writers who ventured into the seductive area of "the social evil" (prostitution) and who, unlike Chekhov, wrote with obvious approval of self-regarding "rescuers of fallen women" ("Aren't I good? I've detected the human being even in a prostitute!")./47/ Gorky had in mind Garshin's sentimental early story *An Incident* (1878), which shows the possible influence of both Gogol and Dostoevsky. Yet Gorky's own portrayal of some of his women characters is not far from Garshin's, Nekrasov's, Dostoevsky's or Kuprin's, since he, too, "had his own sentimental cult of prostitutes, whom he portrayed as spiritually vulnerable creatures, concealing beneath their coarseness the souls of mothers and saints"./48/ Indeed, his early story, *The Hapless Pavel* (1894), contains a situation that is strikingly similar to the climactic scene in Garshin's *An Incident*, even down to the rhetoric, part sentimental, part hysterical, employed by the two men as they plead with their respective fallen women to allow them to perform any deed, however melodramatic or degrading, in order to "rescue" them./49/ But in 1910 Gorky bestowed on Garshin the supreme accolade when, in a letter to P.Maksimov, he linked his name with those of Herzen, Uspensky, Saltykov-Shchedrin and Korolenko as epitomising the sterling qualities of

GARSHIN AND THE EARLY GORKY

the Russian writer, in the oft-quoted reverential phrase: "The Russian writer ... must be treated with redoubled respect, for he is an almost heroic figure, a living vessel of stupendous sincerity and great love"./50/

That Gorky was familiar with Garshin's stories and certainly with *Artists*, is shown by his references to the Populist-oriented artist Riabinin in that work, in *The Disintegration of Personality* (1909), and in *Talks about Craftsmanship* (1930-1)./51/ Curiously, though, there is no record of any comment by him on *The Red Flower* which bears so many striking similarities with his early works, notably *Old Izergil*, *The Song of the Falcon* and *A Mistake*./52/

III

One feature that Garshin and Gorky share with many other "democratic" Russian writers is their perception of literature as a vehicle for arousing the reader's conscience, making him aware of the suffering of the common people and mobilising his resolve to alleviate it. Both writers felt genuine compassion for people (*bol' za liudei, za cheloveka*), and both demonstrated the artistic traps into which such strong social commitment can lead: Garshin could sometimes lapse into maudlin sentimentality, even into near-hysteria, while Gorky, too, often lost control of his material, his language becoming tediously inflated and his stories diffuse and nebulous. These were the defects against which Chekhov warned him. There is evidence of these weaknesses in *A Mistake*, while they are strikingly absent from *The Red Flower*, where, as Mikhailovsky said, "everything is clear, definite and carved out of one piece, not a line could be added or taken away"./53/ But Gorky, too, could write dense prose and did so superbly in the *sketch* (*ocherk*) - *A Procession*/54/ - published in the same year as *A Mistake*. This is a detailed, matter-of-fact account, less than three pages long, of the appalling punishment suffered by a peasant woman caught in adultery, an incident which Gorky witnessed on his way to Tiflis. It is a piece of documentary "disturbing art" of the highest order.

Gorky grew up in "the back alleys of life" and had first-hand experience of the way "the submerged nine-tenths" lived. Garshin's hypersensitive conscience drove him to share the hardships endured by the Russian uniformed peasant by joining the Imperial Army in 1877 as a volunteer private and taking part in the march from Kishinev to the Bulgarian battlefields where he was wounded in action. He wrote about his experiences in several stories and a *sketch*, emphasising the stoicism and humanity of the ordinary soldiers as witnessed by the *intellectual* among them.

Kaun's speculative explanation of the two men's socio-psychological instincts is relevant here. Describing Gorky as "being irresistibly drawn towards men of the fifth estate", he comments:

> Those of a restless introspective nature are familiar with this, temporary or permanent, yearning after a carefree, irresponsible environment, in which to drown their inner voice, still and small but as annoyingly perseverant as a gnat. Vsevolod Garshin ... haunted to death by black melancholy over life's cruelty and injustice, felt at ease, physically and mentally, while serving as a private in the war against Turkey... No wonder that Alexey Peshkov, precociously observant, bloated with an indigestible mass of impressions, experiences, and bookish notions, sought relief in the I-don't-care milieu of submerged humanity"./55/

This quaintly-worded attempt to bracket the two writers has its attractions as another formulation of the *bol' za liudei* motivation; however, because of Garshin's and Gorky's very different social origins, experiences and expectations, Kaun's thesis is not fully valid.

GARSHIN AND THE EARLY GORKY

Bol' za liudei often found expression in an act or stance of *podvig* (heroic deed) which represents a more private and more religious form of "protest" than do the variants of "going to the people". The two strands were, however, often concomitant: perceiving the totality of institutionalised inequality, injustice and cruelty, the "conscious" individual (or "penitent *intelligent*") is shown to perceive the wrongs of the prevailing social order and their consequences in steeply escalating form, regarding them as emanations of a sinister elemental force — "universal evil". Its existence is either not recognised or is tolerated and thereby perpetuated by passive humanity. The *podvizhnik* (hero-martyr) experiences a spiritual initiation and finds the will and strength to combat single-handed the power of evil. He sees himself as a visionary and hero who will struggle to achieve "the impossible dream" — the destruction of evil, the liberation and rebirth of mankind, and the establishment of a new Golden Age, which can be achieved only through the hero's fanatical devotion to the ideal and his voluntary acceptance of martyrdom. This variant on the theme of the Exceptional Individual, so prominent in the works of Garshin and Gorky, can be traced back, via Mikhailovsky (e.g. his *Hero and Crowd*, 1882), to Pisarev and the Utopian Socialists before him.

Several generations of Russian reformers and revolutionaries saw their task in such apocalyptic or "fantastic" terms, and the "fight with evil" became virtually commonplace. Garshin had already displayed such an apocalyptic trait in his childhood:

> ...occasionally this cheerful, carefree schoolboy would suddenly become quiet and fall silent, as though displeased with himself and those around him... He would utter remarks about the need to combat evil and express very strange views on how to achieve happiness for all mankind./56/

Something very similar is on record about Chitadze, who was known as "a youthful idealist and untiring worker for the cause of Loving One's Neighbour, a remarkable young man who dreamed of eradicating evil on earth"./57/

However, this lofty stance too often degenerated into one very different from Christian humility and altruism, though religious imagery and terminology were frequently still employed to express the hero's motivation. Almost inevitably such a *podvig* born of "the Agony of Populist Art", as Billington terms it,/58/ involves the hero's self-elevation above common mankind and a concomitant disregard or even contempt for the humanity for whose sake the lone battle is waged. As the hero's fight becomes increasingly internalised and private, the humanitarian purpose fades from his consciousness and a Nietzschean perception takes over, so that he lives and dies inspired by a vision of himself as one of the Chosen Few, a man of destiny, a redeemer and superman. Thus Garshin's anonymous hero in *The Red Flower* is possessed by an "ecstasy of pride" (*gordelivoe isstuplenie*) as he joins battle with evil, convinced that "he will perish and die, but will die ... the first fighter of mankind, because so far no one had ventured to fight with all the world's evil at once" (VG: 195-6). This quasi-Nietzschean trait is even more evident in Gorky's story, as Mikhailovsky had pointed out.

Gorky's madman is possessed by a heroic vision: "In me there blazes the immortal fire of desire for a heroic deed!" (*Vo mne pylaet bessmertnyi ogon' zhelaniia podviga!*) (I,111), and it is not surprising that both this *podvig* and Kravtsov's vision of future society abound in religious echoes. It is significant that his images and symbols are taken primarily from the Old Testament and Jewish history. He sees himself as a new Moses leading the Israelites out of slavery in Egypt into a new Promised Land. Moses - who led the Exodus and ascended Mount Sinai to receive from Jehovah the Ten Commandments, an inspired and demanding leader unswerving in his purpose despite the hardships facing him and his followers - was an apposite model for Kravtsov's inflated self-image as prophet, teacher and leader. Moreover, in Gorky's time the figure of Moses still featured prominently in both the ecclesiastical and secular traditions, and its symbolism would be recognised by the pious *narod* and secular intelligentsia alike./59/

Other Old Testament imagery employed includes that of Jacob's Ladder (see below), and there are somewhat incongruous references to the writings of St. Augustine and St. John Chrysostom. A similar cultural leap enables Kravtsov to designate his select band as *bratiia*, a term whose meaning is more exclusively monastic than are its English equivalents (fraternity, brotherhood)./60/ The "Castalian fountain of liberty" is a garbled reference to Pythia, Apollo's priestess at Delphi.

Kravtsov excludes from this march towards the new life the likes of Iaroslavtsev, whom at this stage he equates with his enemies - "the Egyptians" - and all those whom he deems spiritually and aesthetically unworthy of liberation and rebirth. His vision is thus highly elitist and exclusive, for it comprises his own select "fraternities" (like the tribes of Israel), and not suffering humanity in general.

In Garshin's story the concept of *podvig* is also heroic: together with *delo* (the cause), it ultimately stands for "initiating revolution",/61/ in marked contrast to its use at the heroico-comical level as "adventure" by one of the characters in *Old Izergil*./62/

Kravtsov also introduces New Testament themes and imagery into his Old

Testament vision. However, "the poor in spirit" here are not the common people of the Sermon of the Mount but "conscious" men like himself, despised and rejected by the rulers of this world: "We, the poor in spirit, shall depart from life sadly" (I,112). In the terms of this world, Kravtsov and his fraternity will be defeated, "...for we shall depart with our shields broken in our hands and without the armour of faith that we shall have lost in the battle!" (I,112). Here, in one of the inverted realities in which the story abounds, Gorky expresses a resurrectionist vision - the poor shall inherit the world, defeat leads to victory, and death to the new life on earth. Garshin had similarly expressed the concept of the "power of the powerless" in his review of an exhibition of Peredvizhnik paintings in 1880. *A propos* of Surikov's canvas *Boiarinia Morozova*, he wrote:

> Yes, great is the power of weakness! If an idea, however bizarre ... takes hold of a man's soul ... if that man is oppressed, in chains, if he is dragged off ... into an underground prison, to his execution, the crowd will always stop and listen to what he has to say (VG: 363-4).

In Garshin's statement there is more altruism than in Kravtsov-Chitadze's, whose despised and defeated outcasts shall return, armed with an invincible weapon (a typically Gorkian concept) - "a strong faith in ourselves, and there is no weapon stronger than that!" (I,111). But Gorky has Iaroslavtsev mentally downgrade the heroic image to the comic by likening the ecstatic visionary to the Pied Piper assembling rats and mice on a river bank. However, the Nietzschean theme of the Select Few gains the upper hand, though it is couched in the terminology of the Sermon on the Mount. Kravtsov continues:

> I want to lead all those men out of life who, despite their stains, are yet the brightest people in life... They are

GARSHIN AND THE EARLY GORKY

perishing from the misery of their loneliness and from being persecuted by you. They are suffocating in the stench of life that you breathe so easily... Let me rescue them! (I,114)

Gradually, Iaroslavtsev is no longer viewed as one of "them" and comes to qualify for participation in the great venture: among those "imprisoned in life" (*v plenu u zhizni*) Kravtsov now includes people "who had wanted to become heroes, and became statisticians and teachers instead" (I,115) - that is, he intends primarily to rescue such "defeated heroes", who historically are former members of The People's Will. By joining "the new heroes", Iaroslavtsev wins the chance of spiritual resurrection.

The *Vita Nuova* will paradoxically be established in the desert. There a novel kind of social institution will be founded, whose highly eccentric title of "Booth of Universal Salvation" (*budka vseobshchego spaseniia*) carries several allusions. Kravtsov stresses that it will be "a booth, not a commune, not a phalanstery, a booth - that's quite legal, surely?" (I, 115). The reference is both to the Tiflis commune and to the tenets of Utopian socialism, the "phalanstery" being the dwelling of the *phalange* in Fourier's ideal social system - the term was adopted by Chernyshevsky and given new content in his *What is To Be Done?* This designation of the new social organisation also appears to echo that of the Salvation Army (*Armiia spaseniia*), which was and is viewed by Russian socialists with suspicion./63/ In this laboured instance of Aesopian language we have another example of heroic-comic imagery.

Kravtsov himself will be the unchallenged Teacher and Leader, and here the visions of Dostoevsky's Shigalev (in *The Devils*) emerge with chilling clarity:

> I shall stand above them and ... teach them all that I know.
> I know a great deal ... for I know everything... With us, the

81

PETER HENRY

Booth of Universal Salvation will tower above all others and on its top, under a glass cupola, I myself shall hover and see to order among those entrusted to me by fate. I shall be severe and fair, though not in the human sense (*ne po-chelovecheskii spravedliv*) (I,116).

Like Dostoevsky's hero who foresaw the advent of fascist totalitarianism, so Gorky's, "having started from the idea of unlimited freedom, ends up with that of unlimited despotism". Kravtsov envisages his own boundless knowledge as a vital historical force and postulates "a higher truth" to which he alone is privy - symptoms of megalomania at the level of solipsism indeed. Here Gorky anticipates both the imagery of Zamiatin's *We* and the role of the all-wise Benefactor in it; while the phrase "*ne po-chelovecheski spravedliv*" implies a superhuman (i.e. divine) justice dispensed by Kravtsov.

He also adumbrates the concept of a world-state that would involve the dissolution of individual states, world revolution, international solidarity and the "struggle against imperialism and its hirelings":

When we have built our kingdom, where all will be in harmony, we shall summon all the spies and all the mighty of the earth and all the stupid nations and we shall say to them: "You persecuted us, but we have built a model of life for all time! Here it is, follow it! We, reborn from the ashes, will go on to create eternally" (I,116).

In a new interpretation of "The poor shall inherit the earth", he, the leader of these erstwhile paupers, shall say to the world: "People, put on garments of light, for the night has vanished and shall not return" (*Liudi, oden'tes' v svetloe, ibo noch' ischezla i ne pridet bol'she*) (I, 116) - a poetic evocation of the Orthodox liturgy.

Kravtsov's aggressive self-elevation has grown by leaps and bounds. He sees himself as "the good genius" and "the eagle of the future". But his grandiose vision infects Iaroslavtsev who has "repented" and, converted to the new teaching, becomes Kravtsov's first disciple. They will ascend together "the ladder of happiness and enter eternal bliss, like the angels in Jacob's dream, as the creators of life, the renewers of the spirit" (I, 117). Iaroslavtsev sees a picture of a road filled with people departing from the prison of life; but for him, unlike for Kravtsov, this is an image in the spirit of the New Testament:

> There were many of them. Among them children ... weeping in the arms of their fathers and mothers. The fathers and mothers walked on silently, covered in dust, in tattered garments, and through their eyes [Iaroslavtsev] could see their souls filled with misery and in rags - the worn-out and tattered souls of people who had suffered much (I,118).

In this evocative but over-written passage, Iaroslavtsev is shown as having acquired a share in divine insight - at the price of accepting the totalitarian authority of the Leader (the *Führer, Duce* or *Vozhd'* of the future): "Ahead of them all strode he, the great man, whom everybody obeyed and to whom everyone looked with hope, and beside whom Iaroslavtsev could see himself" (I,118).

One could, charitably, assume that Gorky, sensing the Nietzschean implications of Kravtsov's programme, introduced the humanitarian theme in a kind of coda voiced by Iaroslavtsev. Thereby Gorky moved in his ambiguous story away from Nietzsche's *Thus Spake Zarathustra* and closer to Wells's modern Utopias, the first of which, incidentally, *The Time Machine*, appeared in 1895, the same year as Gorky's *A Mistake*. Nevertheless, the seminal thought in Kravtsov's vision carries greater emotional force than its "soft" reinterpretation by Iaroslavtsev, and it is the former that dominates the story.

If the above discussion is conjectural, there is one episode in the work where Gorky clearly attempted to reduce its Nietzschean flavour. It

83

occurs when Iaroslavtsev considers the paradoxical axiom that "pity is cruelty" (I,106). This sparks off a memory from his life in the country: a cow had fallen into a ravine, injuring itself badly, and a large crowd of villagers was peering down at it. They were looking at it "less out of compassion than curiosity". He had joined the crowd, the incident being both "interesting and sad". The static scene is animated by the arrival of the village blacksmith Matvei, "tall, stern and stained with coal", carrying a heavy metal bar. He becomes both the crowd's judge and the cow's executioner:

> He surveyed them all with a severe, heavily reproachful look in his eyes, knitted his brows and shaking his head, said loudly: "Fools! What are you looking at?" Then he swung his piece of iron and struck the heifer's head! The sound of the blow was dull and soft, yet the skull split open, and this was very frightening. The heifer was no longer mooing or complaining with its large, limpid eyes of its pain... Matvei went away (I,107).

Iaroslavtsev feels a thrill when Matvei carries out his deed of mercy-killing. The crowd comments: "That's Matvei's way of feeling pity. Perhaps he would do that to someone hopelessly ill. Is that moral or immoral? *It's strong - it's moral and good*" (*Sil'no - moral'no i khorosho*) (I,107; my italics).

Gorky's involvement with "Nietzscheanism" has been the subject of a protracted and sometimes virulent debate, with too many participants producing black-or-white conclusions. How well did he know the German philosopher's writings, did he understand them, and which of them had he read? What did Nietzsche actually mean to him, to his generation and to various Russian commentators? One welcomes Babaian's open verdict that "the question of the young Gorky's involvement with Nietzsche (*nitssheanstvo*) is far from simple"./65/ He reminds us that Gorky told A. Volynsky

GARSHIN AND THE EARLY GORKY

(Flekser) in 1898 that "as far as I know him, I like Nietzsche", and that "the reactionary meaning of his teaching ... was not clear to many"./66/

In the first edition of Gorky's stories, Iaroslavtsev's question, "Is that moral or immoral?", was followed by this compromising comment: "In any case, this is strong, above all it's strong and accordingly it's moral and good" (*Vo vsiakom sluchae eto sil'no, prezhde vsego sil'no i potomu ono moral'no i khorosho*). Critics agree, at least, that Gorky was "prone to admire strength for no other reason than that it exists", as F.M.Borras said à *propos* of this passage./67/ Equally, however, the fact that Gorky removed this sentence from the second and all subsequent editions supports our thesis that he later wished to reduce the ominous implications of Kravtsov's programme.

In Garshin's *Four Days* there is also a remembered episode, strikingly similar to Iaroslavtsev's. The solitary hero-narrator of this story lies dying of his wounds after a minor engagement in the Russo-Turkish War. Longing for, yet fearing, deliverance by death, he recalls the slow, painful death of a little dog after a street accident:

> I was walking down a street, and a bunch of people pulled me up short. The crowd was just standing there and looking silently at a little white bloodstained thing that was whining pitifully It was a nice little dog; it had been run over by a horse-drawn tram. It lay dying, as I am now. A caretaker pushed through the crowd, grabbed the little dog by the scruff of its neck and carried it away. The crowd dispersed (VG: 6).

Garshin-Ivanov draws a parallel between himself and the dying dog. And, like Iaroslavtsev, he is not distressed by what he saw: "That day (when the little dog was run over), I'd been happy. I'd been intoxicated, and with good reason. Don't torment me, memories, leave me alone!" (VG: 6-7) - memories of a day of unclouded happiness. There is a quasi-Nietzschean

85

tone here, in marked contrast to the writer's "normal", highly compassionate attitude, whether to the victims of war or to living organisms generally (e.g. *Attalea Princeps*).

*   *   *   *

Gorky's visionary had cloaked his messianic programme in a transformed version of the Old Testament story, and in so doing had produced a Wellsian prophecy of the twentieth century. By contrast, the prevailing ethos in Garshin's story, in religious terms, is that of the New Testament, whereas the hero's struggle with evil is portrayed with the imagery and symbolism of Zoroastrianism./68/ The hero of *The Red Flower* prepares for martyrdom in accordance with a bizarre yet coherent logic. When, on admission to the hospital, he is taken for a bath,

> absurd thoughts, one more monstrous than the other, whirled in his head. What was this? The Inquisition? A secret place of execution where his enemies had resolved to do away with him? Perhaps it was hell itself? In the end it occurred to him that this was [to be] some kind of ordeal (VG: 186).

He struggles violently as he is immersed in the water - manifestly a travesty of baptism - yet he submits to his "ordeal", and in this heroico-comic re-enactment of the ritual of medieval chivalry he becomes eligible for martyrdom. The Patient now associates himself with "all those martyred before me" (VG: 186) and specifically with the hero-saint George the Dragon-Slayer. The hospital is, in the Patient's consciousness, a microcosm of the world on the eve of Judgment Day, a metaphysical prison where innocent men are forcibly detained. He sees it as his mission to liberate them and believes that liberation will achieve the rebirth of purified mankind:

GARSHIN AND THE EARLY GORKY

Soon, soon, the iron bars will fall asunder and those incarcerated here will go forth and rush to all the ends of the earth, the whole world will shudder, cast off its threadbare mantle and come forth in a miraculous new beauty (VG: 193).

In his "ecstasy of pride" the Patient has acquired powers of omniscience and omnipotence: he can read the thoughts of others and see in things their entire history, and he fills the hospital with "men from all times and all lands. Here were both the living and the dead. Here were the famous and mighty of the world and soldiers killed in the last war who had risen from the dead" (VG: 193).

His mission crystallises into a struggle against universal evil, a private battle in which he expects to die. Although here, too, a Nietzschean echo sounds, the dominant theme is salvation of the world through martyrdom in the manner of Christ. The patient asks the doctor: "Why do you do evil?" (VG: 188) and shouts at the orderlies: "You don't know what you are doing! You are doomed!... Let me complete my task!... Then it will be all over, everything will be saved. I would send you, but only I can do this" (VG: 197). He is vitally concerned to absorb the poppy's deadly juices into his own body and thereby prevent them from pouring into the world as the flower expires. In this self-immolatory altruism lies the crucial difference between Garshin's hero and Kravtsov with his solipsist, totalitarian vision.

IV

There can be little doubt that the portrait of Kravtsov and his Utopian programme are the core of the story, and that Iaroslavtsev is conceived essentially as a foil to Kravtsov. However, Iaroslavtsev's visit to

87

PETER HENRY

Kravtsov does not occur until after a third of the work. The first third is devoted almost exclusively to Iaroslavtsev's mental condition which is portrayed in considerable, even laborious detail. One is therefore not justified in dismissing the first third of the story as an extended introduction, let alone in ignoring it as some commentators do.

The character of Iaroslavtsev, artistically only a qualified success, is nevertheless of considerable relevance for Gorky and his time. It is the portrait of a disillusioned dreamer alienated by the stagnation of contemporary life. A representative of the present "hero-less age" (*bezgeroinoe vremia*) who reluctantly conforms with the mundane ideology of Little Deeds (*malye dela*), he is filled with nostalgia for the heroic past and with fear of an uncertain future. He can thus be seen as a former Populist who, after 1881, gave up the cause of insurrection and, like Garshin's Riabinin, became a rural teacher in order to conduct peaceful socialist propaganda among the people. Iaroslavtsev's two occupations - those of teacher and statistician - show that he still is, or was, socially concerned; moreover, those were the very occupations chosen by many former members of Land and Freedom and The People's Will.

Iaroslavtsev is a thoroughly "cerebral" character of the kind disliked by Korolenko and Mikhailovsky; he is also the work's only character who is not described physically, whereas even minor figures like Minorny, Liakhov and Iaroslavtsev's landlady are so described and their movements and appearance recorded in often excessive detail. Though his mental and psychological condition is amply demonstrated, no biographical information is provided, and in this sense he appears as a more truly "fictional" character than Kravtsov. In fact, he is a composite portrait based partly, as

GARSHIN AND THE YOUNG GORKY

stated, on a Tiflis acquaintance, partly on a Russian telegraphist whom Gorky met in 1889 and who provided the surname,/69/ and partly on several of the author's own character traits. That shaping the story gave Gorky much trouble is known from his own remarks and from the various drafts which show how many changes he made before he was satisfied with the final text./70/ Most of his structural problems arose from the Iaroslavtsev component which appears to have been grafted on to the "front" of the main story.

Whilst dealing with the general theme of mental disorder, the Iaroslavtsev theme is concerned not with heroic eccentricity (Kravtsov), but with the anxieties of a "little man" suffering from persecution mania. This accounts partly for the two levels of the narrative and for its tonality, discussed by B.V.Mikhailovsky./71/ Whereas Kravtsov's ironic and eccentric humour is directed at the external world, Iaroslavtsev's is aimed largely at himself, self-parodying and self-deprecatory in the manner of a man suffering from insecurity and loss of faith.

Iaroslavtsev functions on one level as observer, commentator and foil, and on another as the frustrated idealist who rediscovers a cause, however Utopian, and finds a leader, however solipsist and uncompromising, to follow. Earlier, he is shown as intimidated by the forces that restrict his existence, yet he is equally afraid of any change for the better. He dare not even dream of a happier life, let alone of ways, however improbable, of achieving a transformation in himself or his surroundings. At the same time he is aware of the imminence of change, sensing an air of expectancy everywhere: "The dust-covered leaves of trees ... were not stirring; everything was motionless and ... expecting some kind of tremor" (I,105).

He believes he has been denied the right to think or dream - thought itself seems a dangerous, even prohibited activity which a sinister external authority can detect. Yet "oppressive and disturbing thoughts" assail him, many of them amorphous and devoid of purpose. They are the dominant elements of his existence and, while terrified of them, he has come to welcome their advent as he lies, Oblomov-like, on his couch, falling easy prey to their onslaughts. "Like millstones, they crush all that is good and serene in his life, and all that was given to him by the dream [mechta - the vision of a happier life] is changed into dry, colourless, acrid dust" (I,98).

He expects the emergence of some "terrible fact", "something stern and triumphant" that will stand by his couch and say to him: "I can see what you are thinking about!... I am aware of the minutest convolutions of your brain" (I,98). In Gorky's vocabulary "fact" was an inert, static concept. "Facts aren't the essence, one's moods are. Facts are nothing but trash and rubbish", says the main character in his story *A Rascal*, also published in 1898 (IV,54). Kravtsov's programme, on the other hand, belongs in the complex of "moods"/"obsessions" (*nastroeniia*), thoughts, dreams and "the comforting lie", "the deception that uplifts you" (*uteshitel'naia lozh'*, *vozvyshaiushchii obman*). Iaroslavtsev, by contrast, hoping that "thought" will degenerate into mere "fact", further demonstrates his timidity. He fears that the sinister "fact" which he dare not or cannot identify is capable of rebirth and metamorphosis, and that it will become monstrous and devour him. This vagueness contrasts with the heroic treatment of thoughts and dreams by Kravtsov, for whom the "idea" is a welcome, life-giving force.

GARSHIN AND THE EARLY GORKY

Similarly, Garshin's Patient was capable of much greater precision than Iaroslavtsev when formulating his bizarre "thought"; the red poppy with its various attributes – serpentine, poisonous, electrical, some of them antinomous – represented his "enemy":

> That red flower had absorbed all the evil of the world. He *knew* that opium was made from poppies; it was perhaps *this thought*, growing and assuming monstrous shapes, that *had caused him to create* this frightening, fantastic spectre (VG: 195; my italics)

In what is a telling example of the *pokazalos' – okazalos'* "technique" that has been defined as one of the hallmarks of literary impressionism,/72/ Garshin's hero does not leave his "fantastic spectre" unnamed, without form or definition. On the contrary, he progressively endows it with the hallucinatory equivalents of flesh and blood and gives it an identity – "it was Ahriman, the antithesis of God" (VG: 195) – a being that he can oppose and destroy in his "spectral fight". For Iaroslavtsev thoughts were uncontrollable, hostile forces; for Garshin's Patient and for Kravtsov they become powerful weapons which enable them to mobilise their will to fight for the fulfilment of their visions – the destruction of evil on earth, the miraculous transformation of man and the establishment of a new order.

Both stories demonstrate the characteristic Russian emphasis on the primacy of the "idea" (*ideia, mysl'*) and its creative potential. The idea mobilises consciousness, begets the deed and thus constitutes a material and historical force. Conversely, by annihilating the opponent's idea, you disarm him. Garshin had expressed this concept in his agitated letter to Loris-Melikov in 1880, urging him to oppose the idea of violence with that of all-forgiveness – "*to put to death* the idea (*kaznit' ideiu*) that has... shed so much blood and so many tears of both innocent and guilty men"./73/

PETER HENRY

The energising force of ideas is expressed by Garshin's Patient when he explains to the doctor that "a person who has reached the stage where he has a great thought in his soul, a general thought - doesn't mind where he lives, what he feels. Even whether to live or not to live..." (VG: 188-9). The "general thought" he has discovered is that "time and space are myths" and, thus powerfully armed, the Patient is capable of performing miracles of eschatological proportions. Later he concretises his abstract concept in the potent, if bizarre, image of cosmic evil and its corollary - his mission to destroy it.

Gorky takes the animisation and concretisation of thoughts much further, and it is here that one detects the "decadent" flavour of, for example, some of Leonid Andreev's writings. Iaroslavtsev spends much mental energy on identifying the origins and nature of ideas, and Gorky employs a rich variety of visual, tactile and sound images to endow his hero's thought processes with tangible shape, thereby enabling him to gain some control over them. In this he illustrates a natural human tendency away from the amorphous towards definition, but since he does not allow his soliloquising hero to sacrifice any detail, many of these cerebral images suffer from being too elaborate and wearying by their frequency. (It was this propensity towards the prolix that marred much of Gorky's early writing, a flaw which Chekhov criticised as "lack of restraint"). The "birth of thought", for instance, is conveyed in terms of colour, moisture, temperature and corrosion: "Giving everything a dark colouring, moist and cold like autumn clouds, they left behind them the corrosion of melancholy and dull indifference in his soul" (I,97). Thoughts are living, generally repulsive organisms whose growth is impervious to all attempts

GARSHIN AND THE EARLY GORKY

to control them. While in Garshin's story *A Night* (1880) thought is a "maggot" nibbling away at the hero's soul (VG: 115), thoughts "crawl" behind Iaroslavtsev wherever he goes, giving him no peace until he surrenders to them. The tyranny of thoughts is conveyed in a variety of sensory images. In Iaroslavtsev's head everything appears in colours - round spots of yellow, blue and red that whirl before his eyes. When he gains momentary relief from his fear of madness by believing that Kravtsov, and not he, is mad,

> something strange happened to this paltry thought: it descended into a dark pothole, losing sight of the horizons; then it would arise to somewhere high and free, encompassing the vast space; it would fly along slowly and lazily as though growing faint; then it would rapidly speed to somewhere, knocking into a variety of objects on the way; and again it seemed to fall down and vanish (I,112).

In a vain attempt to halt the process of disintegration, Iaroslavtsev likens his mind to the workings of a mechanical contraption - "a mass of spiral springs [is] contracting and expanding, endowing each other with power and movement" (I,103). However, this complex yet orderly system degenerates into chaos when one of the springs contracts and expands more powerfully than the others. The image obviously carries further metaphorical overtones and it strongly echoes that of the mechanical-industrial hell in Riabinin's nightmare in Garshin's *Artists* (VG: 87-8).

*   *   *   *

For both Garshin's and Gorky's sick heroes the existence of a powerful "enemy" is of crucial importance; if he does not exist, he has to be invented. (Garshin's story explicitly posits a Manichean dualism, Gorky's does so by implication). That enemy is ubiquitous, wily and capable of disguise, while his constant purpose is to prevent the hero from engaging in his lofty mission. The enemy can conceal himself in the hero's caring friends (*A Mistake*) or in the hospital staff who are concerned that the sick man does not exhaust or injure himself (*The Red Flower*). In the Patient's perception these good people do this because they have been blinded by the evil one: "Oh you unhappy ones!" he thought, "You can't see, you've become so blind that you even protect him" (VG: 193). These unwitting agents of evil are unaware of the mortal dangers lurking in the world and in fact contribute to the advent of cosmic disaster.

Garshin's hero had initially, in the bathroom episode, perceived his enemies in the hospital attendants, but gradually the diffuse plural ("his enemies") is imperceptibly concentrated in a potent single being ("his enemy"), who performs a much more sinister task than physically restraining him. With the logic of madness the Patient now perceives a metaphysical principle - evil - as his private enemy, whom he alone has identified in the red poppy and whom he alone is prepared to fight to the death. When he burns the first of the three poppies in the bathroom stove, he watches as "*his* enemy hissed and shrivelled" (VG: 196). During his "spectral struggle" he "hurled curses at *his* enemy" (VG: 196; my italics), whom he has identified as "Ahriman", the Satan-figure in Zoroastrian theology, the counter to Ormazd, the God of Light.

Kravtsov, too, initially sees his colleague who looks after him, as an "enemy". He abuses him, calling him a "fool" and "a vile grimace of Nature" (I,110). Later he calls him "Judas", suspecting that Iaroslavtsev has been paid by the authorities to spy on him and discover his great secret. But Kravtsov does not seek to join the ranks of earlier hero-martyrs.

GARSHIN AND THE EARLY GORKY

Instead he sees himself as a secular prophet, as the sole, unaided creator of a new world, and as its new Adam. In these respects the philosophical structure of *A Mistake* differs markedly from that of *The Red Flower*.

V

Critics have not noted the fact that the introduction of Iaroslavtsev led to another structural change - the transfer of the work's action from the Caucasus to an unnamed provincial town "somewhere in Russia". The setting includes no exotic scenery and no mountains, and all the characters are Russian. (Gorky also changed the time from mid-winter to high summer). An objective reason for the change of location was the fact that the story was written three years later, in Nizhny-Novgorod, yet this change served a useful artistic purpose: the "exotic" is restricted to the figure of Kravtsov and his fantastic mission, further highlighted by the anonymous setting. Garshin's story is set "somewhere in the Ukraine", while time, place and personal names are kept obscure. Stylistically, both stories reveal a rich use of colours - in Garshin's red, black and white predominate, while Gorky's range is much more extravagant. Since the main action of both works occurs at night, there is extensive use of light and shade; not surprisingly in these stories about lunatics, the moon - and the stars - are very prominent and richly symbolic. What surprises, though, is that in a work about statisticians so little use is made of number symbolism (in which *The Red Flower* abounds) - with one important exception: the triple use of the word *oshibka*, the title of Gorky's complex and enigmatic story.

What is this "mistake"? The word is Iaroslavtsev's and it first occurs as he ponders the paradox "pity = cruelty": "I must write an article about this - then there will be one mistake less" (I,106). It next occurs when he discovers that Kravtsov's face has not been disfigured by his illness but is quite calm: "[Iaroslavtsev] stepped back and smiled, supremely pleased at his mistake" (I,108). At its third and final mention, "mistake" is used on a different plane altogether. When colleagues and medical personnel come to take Kravtsov to the asylum, Iaroslavtsev exclaims: "But gentlemen! What are you doing? This is a mistake! You think he is mad? That's an offensive mistake, gentlemen! An insulting mistake!" (I,120). (The triple use of the word was no doubt deliberate). "He is no madman... It's we who are becoming scoundrels, dying morally, we are dying the death of madness ... dying in a mean and vulgar way" (I,120). There follows a philippic against bourgeois society that was to be powerfully developed in *Foma Gordeev* a few years later, where the equally "mad" Foma attacks the madness of society only to be pronounced "insane" by the merchants around him. Gorky's and Garshin's mad heroes see the world as absurd but they do not deny its existence - they defy it.

So Iaroslavtsev and his inspired leader are "mad", but *ipso facto* they have become heroic geniuses who have divined the future, predicting a life in terms that the authorities find incomprehensible and therefore too dangerous to tolerate. The latter resort to the violence at their disposal by incarcerating the men in an asylum. And it is tragically poignant that Iaroslavtsev now reverts to his earlier submissive stance ("One has to submit") (I,99), for he says meekly: "Forgive me, gentlemen! *You are right because there are many of you!* (*Vy pravy, tak kak vas mnogo!*). I do not question your right..." (I,121; my italics), and he "submissively sat on a

GARSHIN AND THE EARLY GORKY

chair, in accordance with the doctor's instructions (I,121). For Iaroslavtsev, even after his initiation into Kravtsov's "great secret", nothing has changed: might is right and there is no room for the "truth" of a dissident minority.

*   *   *   *

While *The Red Flower* is, in a sense, timeless — the Patient's opening declaration about the impending "inquiry" (*reviziia*) is made in the name of Peter the Great — Gorky's story contains explicit references to the current socio-political and cultural situation. Kravtsov asserts polemically that "demonism, symbolism and other unhealthy forms of thought are an essential reaction against the spread of materialism", and that "materialism will be certain soon to lose its credit with all thinking people" (I, 103). A latter-day romantic, he argues that "the cause of the present instability of thought is the evanescence of idealism. Those who drove romanticism out of life have stripped us naked" (I,103). Beyond the utilitarianism and pragmatic aspirations of the materialists and other non-romantics there is a higher truth. The crux of the problem is society's indifference to its own spiritual decline. Salvation can be achieved only by a new leadership, a new aristocracy — Kravtsov's "fraternity" that strongly suggests a party or, indeed, the Party, led by someone with an indomitable will to power. The "trivia of life", Saltykov-Shchedrin's *melochi zhizni*, must and will be swept away by a new élite such as that envisaged by Kravtsov, whose creator had entered this world "in order to disagree". Gorky's heroes have divined that the normal was abnormal and the healthy man basically stupid, content to live by surface realities;

the sick man was the new man of destiny.

In *A Mistake* the link between insanity and genius is shown in provocative fashion, their causes being seen as identical: both derive from an exclusive preoccupation with an idea. Iaroslavtsev is aware that madness is no mere illness: "Supposing [Kravtsov] has become a genius?... It has been proved that geniuses are lunatics. No-one has told us how geniuses are created. Perhaps by going mad, by surrendering into slavery to an idea..." (I,104). Garshin's Riabinin had become a slave to the idea of the hero-martyrdom of art (*podvig iskusstva*), his Patient to that of his confrontation with cosmic evil. Chekhov's Garshin-Vasiliev in *The Breakdown* (1888) saw his task in fighting social evil by *apostol'stvo*, that is, by practically preventing men from entering the Alley of Shame. Garshin, Chekhov and Gorky, thus portraying the essence of *podvizhnichestvo*, would have agreed with R.D.Laing that "our 'normal', 'adjusted' state is too often the abdication of ecstasy, the betrayal of our true potentialities.. many of us are only too successful in acquiring a false self to adapt to false realities"./74/

Garshin's and Gorky's visionaries thus rightfully belong in the gallery of nineteenth-century social dreamers, reformers and revolutionaries. Since their programmes and visions inevitably posed a threat to the status quo, they were ridiculed, declared insane and rendered impotent. In real life there was Robert Owen who, with his co-operative schemes in New Lanark, was held to be insane. (Gorky had Owen's portrait in his room in Kazan in 1887). In literature, Byron in *Don Juan*, Heine in *Atta Troll*, Béranger in *Les Foux*, and others paid tribute to these despised heroes of the spirit who would wear their fool's caps gladly. In fact, of course, it was contemporary society that was "insane" - the Bedlam of the world - but only the demented visionaries were aware of it./75/

Gorky's celebrated phrase *Bezumstvu khrabrykh poem my pesniu* ("We sing a hymn to the madness of the brave"), taken from *The Song of the Falcon*, also published in 1895, refers to the "heroic madness" of Kravtsov, Danko and other romantic heroes in his early works; and it is equally applicable to the hero of *The Red Flower*. From such inspired madness in a leader-figure a Utopian or messianic vision would emerge, which in turn was to lead to radical social change - revolution.

The two stories differ in tone, in their basic structure and their parameters; neither is exclusively a "psychiatric study" and both are "hymns to the madness of the brave". The Soviet Gorky specialist Gruzdev was only partly right when he asserted that *A Mistake* "was aimed against *The Red Flower*" and that Gorky's story was "not derivative, but polemical", implying that Kravtsov was superior to the Patient as a lone hero seeking to annihilate the world's evil./76/ Nor was Mikhailovsky entirely right when he said that *A Mistake* "stands on its own in Mr Gorky's two slim volumes". While its *siuzhet* is unique in Gorky's early works, its message is akin to that of *The Finch and the Woodpecker*, *Old Izergil* and *The Song of the Falcon*. Like them, it expresses the young author's faith in Man (or rather, his cult of the strong man) and his belief in the need for the "uplifting deception". Like Garshin's confessional tale and many of Chekhov's stories of the time, it is a telling statement on the *malaise* of the age. And, like *The Red Flower*, *A Mistake* is another original tribute to the sanctity of *podvig* and *podvizhniki*, in whom Russian life and literature were particularly rich at the time. Despite its structural and other

PETER HENRY

flaws, Gorky's elusive and highly provocative asylum story deserves to be known in the English-speaking world./77/

NOTES

Quotations from Gorky's works are normally taken from the recent Academy edition: M.Gor'kii, *Polnoe sobranie sochinenii: khudozhestvennye proizvedeniia v dvadtsati piati tomakh* (Moscow, 1968-); references to this edition are given in the text as volume no. + page no. (e.g. I,169). References to Gorky's *Sobranie sochinenii v 30-i tomakh* (Moscow, 1953) are incorporated in the notes as *SS* + volume no. + page no. (e.g. *SS*: XXIII,43). Quotations from and references to Garshin's works are taken from: V.M.Garshin, *Sochineniia* (Moscow, 1955); they are shown as *VG* followed by page no. (e.g. *VG*: 193).

1. The story has, however, been discussed in the following articles: E.P. Sakharova, "'Chernyi monakh' A.P.Chekhova i 'Oshibka' M.Gor'kogo", in *A.P.Chekhov: sbornik statei i materialov* (Rostov-na-Donu, 1959), pp. 233-51; and B.V.Mikhailovskii, "Iz etiudov o romantizme rannego Gor'kogo", in *O khudozhestvennom masterstve M.Gor'kogo; sbornik statei* (Moscow, 1960), pp.5-71 ("Rasskaz 'Oshibka'", pp.43-71).
2. (i) "O g. Maksime Gor'kom i ego geroiakh", in *Russkoe bogatstvo*, No.9 (1898); (ii) "Eshche o g. Maksime Gor'kom i ego geroiakh", *ibid.*, No. 10. Reprinted in N.K.Mikhailovskii, *Otkliki* (St. Petersburg, 1905), Vol. 2, pp.337-59 and 360-94 respectively.
3. *Oshibka: epizod,* first published in *Russkaia mysl'*, No.9 (1895), 119-44. It was included in M.Gor'kii, *Ocherki i rasskazy* (St. Petersburg, 1898), Vol.2; in the second edition the subtitle was dropped. (See S.Balukhatyi, *Literaturnaia rabota M.Gor'kogo: spisok pervopechatnykh tekstov i avtorizirovannykh izdanii* (Moscow-Leningrad, 1936), p.16).
4. *Otkliki*, *op. cit.*, pp.390-3.
5. *Ibid.*, p.390.
6. *Samarskaia gazeta*, 13 and 16 April, 1896 (*SS*: XXIII,124-37).
7. *Otkliki, op cit.*, p.393.
8. On Gorky in Georgia, see, for example: E.Babaian, *Rannii Gor'kii: u ideinykh istokov tvorchestva* (Moscow, 1973); I.Gruzdev, *Gor'kii i ego vremia, 1868-1896*, 3rd edn. (Moscow, 1962); V.Imedadze, *Gor'kii v Gruzii* (Tbilisi, 1948); A.Kaliuzhnyi, "Staryi drug", in *M.Gor'kii v vospominaniiakh sovremennikov*, ed. N.L.Brodskii (Moscow, 1955), pp.87-90; S.I. Mitskevich, "Iz vstrech s molodym Gor'kim", *ibid.*, pp.91-4; B.Piradov, *U istokov tvorchestva Maksima Gor'kogo (1891-92)* (Tbilisi, 1957), and *Na rubezhe: M.Gor'kii v Gruzii nakanune revoliutsii 1905 goda* (Tbilisi, 1975); and N.Pleshchunov, *Maksim Gor'kii i Kavkaz* (Baku, 1939). See also Filia Holtzmann, *The Young Maxim Gorky - 1868-1902* (New York, 1948) and Alexander Kaun, *Maxim Gorky and His Russia* (New York, 1931; re-issued 1968).
9. See, for example, his statement on the tenth anniversary of the establishment of Soviet Georgia in 1931 (*SS*: XXV,4-14).

GARSHIN AND THE EARLY GORKY

10. Gruzdev, *op. cit.*, p.347.
11. First published in *Otechestvennye zapiski*, No.9 (1879), 103-18. As Dedov, the protagonist in *Artists*, explains to Riabinin, "...it's hellish work. The *glukhar'* sits inside the boiler and holds the rivet from inside with a pair of pliers and presses his chest against them with all his might, while the boilersmith, outside, hammers away at the rivet to flatten its head" (*VG*: 80).
12. St. Petersburg, 12 January, 1872; published in V.M.Garshin, *Polnoe sobranie sochinenii v trekh tomakh* (Moscow-Leningrad, 1934), Vol.3: *Pis'ma*, p.424 (henceforth cited as *Pis'ma*).
13. 23 October, 1925 (*SS*: XXIX,446-7). The quotations are taken from Kaun, *op. cit.*, p.221.
14. V.Imedadze demolishes the case for Kaliuzhny's exclusive role in Gorky's decision to become a writer (see Imedadze, *op. cit.*, pp.42-5).
15. Thus, in his valuable, if flawed book on Gorky, Kaun wrote: "Kalyuzhny's pamphlet protests against the statement of I.A.Gruzdev (author of a biographical sketch of Gorky) to the effect that Kalyuzhny locked up Alexey in his room and made him write his story. 'Ridiculous and absurd', exclaims the Tiflis pamphlet. Yet Gorky ... told me that Kalyuzhny, after hearing the story of Makar Chudra, locked him up in his room and made him write down his narrative". (A.Kaun, *op. cit.*, p.220). This account has been refuted by Imedadze (*op. cit.*, p.42).
16. Arkhiv A.M.Gor'kogo, MoG-5-9-1, quoted in *PSS*: I,530. Much essential background information on the story is given here (pp.529-37).
17. In *Otechestvennye zapiski*, No.11, pt.2 (1882), 35-6. On Nikoladze, see A.K.Nikoladze, *Russko-gruzinskie literaturnye sviazi* (Tbilisi, 1965).
18. On echoes of Garshin's floral symbolism in Gorky's early stories, see Peter Henry, "Imagery of *podvig* and *podvizhnichestvo* in the Works of Garshin and the Early Gor'ky", in *The Slavonic and East European Review*, 61 (1983), 147-9 and 156-9.
19. In *Novoe obozrenie*, No.6559 (1903), and *Bakinskie izvestiia*, No.13 (1903), quoted in Gruzdev, *op. cit.*, p.675.
20. See *PSS*: I,532.
21. Letter to Gruzdev, quoted in the above (p.531) and in B.V.Mikhailovskii, *op. cit.*, pp.45-6.
22. Letter to Gruzdev, quoted in *PSS*: I,531.
23. *Bakinskie izvestiia*, No.13 (16 January, 1903), quoted in Imedadze, *op. cit.*, p.55, and in the above, pp.530-1.
24. N.Kara-Murza, in Arkhiv A.M.Gor'kogo, MoG-5-6-1, quoted in *PSS*: I,531; cf. Imedadze, *op cit.*, pp.55-6.
25. Letter to V.A.Fausek, 9 July, 1883, in *Pis'ma*, p.297.
26. "Garshin wrote ... to Loris ... condemning terrorism, but beseeching Loris to pardon Mlodetsky as a sign of moral greatness and the first step in the creation of a new social order. Two letters and a visit could not dissuade Loris from the hanging of Mlodetsky ..." (James H. Billington, *Mikhailovsky and Russian Populism* (Oxford, 1958), pp.116-7. See also Peter Henry, *A Hamlet of his Time: Vsevolod Garshin, the Man, his Works and his Milieu* (Oxford, 1983), pp.106-14).
27. "Vospominaniia V.I.Bibikova", in *Polnoe sobranie sochinenii V.M.Garshina* (St. Petersburg, 1910), p.76.
28. For comments on *A Mistake* published in 1895 and 1898, see *PSS*: I,534-7,

PETER HENRY

and *Russkaia literatura kontsa XIX-nachala XXv: devianostye gody*, ed. B.A.Bialik (Moscow, 1968), p.334. For Mikhailovsky's and Korolenko's comments, see notes 2 and 35 respectively. For contemporary Garshin criticism, see G.A.Bialyi, *V.M.Garshin i literaturnaia bor'ba vos'midesiatykh godov* (Moscow-Leningrad, 1937), Ch.5, and O.Tudge, "V.M.Garshin (1855-1888) and His Works in Russian and Soviet Literary Criticism", B.Litt. Dissertation, Oxford, 1974.

29. *Krasnyi tsvetok*, in *Otechestvennye zapiski*, No.10 (1883), 297-310. Garshin dedicated the story to his mentor Turgenev, who had died shortly before the story's publication.
30. For publication details, see note 3. Though it is regularly asserted that the story has been included in all editions of Gorky's works since the 1898 edition, this is not the case: it is absent, for instance, from the 1972 edition of *Izbrannye proizvedeniia v trekh tomakh: rasskazy i povesti* (Moscow).
31. Published by Editions Kra (Paris, 1929), p.128.
32. D.S.Mirsky, *History of Russian Literature* (London, 1949), p.336.
33. See, for instance, B.V.Mikhailovskii, *op. cit.*, pp.52-5, and *PSS*: I,535.
34. See especially E.P.Sakharova, *op. cit.* (see note 1).
35. V.G.Korolenko, *Izbrannye pis'ma* (Moscow, 1936), Vol.3, p.91.
36. B.V.Mikhailovskii, *op. cit.*, p.44.
37. In *Russkii rasskaz kontsa XIX-nachala XX veka*, ed. B.A.Bialik (Leningrad, 1979), p.156.
38. Letter to D.Ovsianiko-Kulikovskii, late February, 1912, in *M.Gor'kii: materialy i issledovaniia*, (Literaturnyi arkhiv, Vol.3), ed. S.D.Balukhatyi and V.A.Vvedenskii (Moscow-Leningrad, 1941), p.146. The article on Garshin in Vol.4 (pp.335-61) of Ovsianiko-Kulikovskii's *Istoriia russkoi literatury* (Moscow, 1910), is by Korolenko.
39. Letter to I.I.Ionov, December, 1930, in *Letopis' zhizni i tvorchestva A.M.Gor'kogo*, ed. B.A.Bialik (Moscow, 1960), Vol.4: *1930-1936*, p.167.
40. "Allegorii Olivii Shreiner", in M.Gor'kii, *Nesobrannye literaturnokriticheskie stat'i*, ed. S.M.Breitburg (Moscow, 1941), p.34. *Skazanie o gordom Aggee* is here wrongly attributed to Korolenko; this was rectified in *Russkie pisateli o literaturnom trude*, ed. B.Meilakh (Leningrad 1954), Vol.4, p.111.
41. Letter to F.A.Braun, in *Letopis' zhizni i tvorchestva A.M.Gor'kogo*, ed. B.A.Bialik (Moscow, 1959), Vol.3: *1917-1929*, p.365.
42. Letter from Capri, December, 1909, in M.Gor'kii, *Pis'ma k E.P.Peshkovoi, 1906-1932*, (Arkhiv A.M.Gor'kogo, Vol.9), ed. N.N.Zhegalov (Moscow, 1966), p.83.
43. In "N.E.Karonin-Petropavlovskii", 1911 (*PSS*: XI,72).
44. "Gamlet nashikh dnei", in *Russkoe bogatstvo*, No.2 (1882), reprinted in V.M.Garshin, *Polnoe sobranie sochinenii* (St. Petersburg, 1910), pp.539-50.
45. "Pis'ma P.F.Iakubovicha", in *M.Gor'kii: materialy i issledovaniia*, (Literaturnyi arkhiv, Vol.2), ed. S.D.Balukhatyi and V.A.Desnitskii (Moscow, 1936), p.365.
46. "K pobede i tvorchestvu", in his *Nesobrannye literaturno-kriticheskie stat'i*, p.157.
47. M.Gor'kii, *Istoriia russkoi literatury*, ed. I.K.Luppol (Moscow, 1936), p.266.

48. Henry, *A Hamlet of his Time*, op. cit., p.71.
49. *PSS*: I,402. On this, see the above, pp.73-4 and note 17 on p.350.
50. "K russkomu pisateliu ... nado otnosit'sia vdvoine uvazhitel'no, ibo eto est' litso pochti geroicheskoe, izumitel'noi iskrennosti i velikoi liubvi sosud zhivoi", 23 December, 1910, in N.L.Brodskii (ed.), *op. cit.*, p.313.
51. *SS*: XXIV,61-2; XXV,304.
52. See Henry, "Imagery of *podvig*", op. cit., pp.147-8, 156-9.
53. In "Palata No.6", in *Sluchainye zametki*, *Russkie vedomosti*, 4 December, 1892.
54. *PSS*: II,57-60.
55. Kaun, op. cit., p.132.
56. A.Nalimov, "Garshin-gimnazist", in *Zadushevnoe slovo* (St. Petersburg, 1908), p.349.
57. S.A.Vartaniants, "M.Gor'kii v Tiflise", in *Bakinskie izvestiia*, No.13 (16/29 January, 1903); quoted in B.V.Mikhailovskii, op. cit., p.47.
58. J.Billington, *The Icon and the Axe: An Interpretive History of Russian Culture* (New York, 1970), pp.402-03.
59. On the figure of Moses in the Russian Orthodox tradition, see *ibid.*, pp.8-9, 73, 75, 131 and 323.
60. "Bratiia - vse chleny monasheskoi obshchiny", *Sovetskii entsiklopedicheskii slovar'* (Moscow, 1980), p.167. Standard language dictionaries give the non-monastic meaning as secondary. One is tempted to suspect here a cryptic pun based on phonetic (and graphemic) similarity - *bratiia* : *partiia*.
61. Henry, *A Hamlet of his Time*, op. cit., pp.298-301.
62. The reference is to Izergil's past lover, the battle-scarred Pole: "He loved heroic exploits. And when a man loves heroic exploits, he always knows how to perform them and will find places where this can be done. In life there is always room for heroic exploits. He is ready to go to the end of the world, '*chtoby delat' chto-nibud'*'" (*PSS*: I,87). Danko's *podvig*, by contrast, is unambiguously heroic, with a marked Nietzschean aspect.
63. See, for example, *Entsiklopedicheskii slovar'* (Moscow, 1953), Vol.1, p.99: "The Salvation Army is an international reactionary Christian philanthropic organisation ... organised along military lines. Conducts slanderous anti-Soviet propaganda and is one of the weapons of the reactionary aggressive policies of the Anglo-American imperialists".
64. This is a case of parallel development, not of the influence of one on the other. Gorky and Wells did not meet until 1906. On Gorky and Wells, see W.Harrison, "H.G.Wells's View of Russia", in *Scottish Slavonic Review*, 7 (Autumn, 1986), 49-68.
65. Babaian, op. cit., p.209.
66. A.Ninov, "V bor'be za Gor'kogo", in *Zvezda*, No.3 (1958), 191, quoted by Babaian, op. cit., p.213.
67. F.M.Borras, *Maxim Gorky the Writer: An Interpretation* (Oxford, 1967), p.84.
68. Henry, *A Hamlet of his Time*, op. cit., pp.162-4 and 362-3, notes 28-30. See also A.Latynina, *Vsevolod Garshin: tvorchestvo i sud'ba* (Moscow, 1986), p.159.
69. *Letopis' zhizni i tvorchestva A.M.Gor'kogo*, ed. K.D.Muratova (Moscow,

1958), Vol.1: *1868-1907*, pp.62, 63.
70. See M.Gor'kii, *Polnoe sobranie sochinenii: varianty k tomam I-V, 1885-1907* (Moscow, 1974), pp.53-64.
71. Mikhailovskii, *op. cit.*, pp.55-8.
72. See Peter M.Bitsilli, *Chekhov's Art: A Stylistic Analysis*, tr. T.Clyman and E.Cruise (Ann Arbor, 1983), pp.53-9; K.D.Kramer, "Impressionist Tendencies in the Work of Vsevolod Garšin", in *American Contributions to the Seventh International Congress of Slavists*, ed. V.Terras ('s Gravenhage, 1973), Vol.2, pp.339-48; and V.B.Kataev, *Proza Chekhova: problemy i interpretatsii* (Moscow, 1979), pp.21-9.
73. *Pis'ma*, p.207.
74. *The Divided Self: An Existential Study in Sanity and Normality* (Harmondsworth, 1965), p.12.
75. See Mikhailovskii, *op. cit.*, pp.48-52.
76. Gruzdev, *op. cit.*, p.465.
77. By 1960, translations of *Oshibka* had been published in nine foreign languages - Bulgarian (2), Serbo-Croat (3), Hungarian (2), German (3) and one each in Czech, Slovak, Romanian, French and Chinese. The story has not been translated into English. (See *Proizvedeniia A.M.Gor'kogo v perevodakh na inostrannye iazyki. Otdel'nye zarubezhnye izdaniia, 1900-1955: bibliograficheskii ukazatel'* (Moscow, 1958), pp.354-5; A. Ettlinger and J.Gladstone, *Bibliography of Russian Literature in English Translation to 1945* (London, 1972); and R.Lewanski, *The Literatures of the World in English Translation: A Bibliography. Vol.II: The Slavic Literatures* (New York, 1971); Garth M.Terry, *Maxim Gorky in English: A Bibliography 1868-1936-1986* (Cotgrave, Nottingham, 1986), pp.9-14). *Krasnyi tsvetok* has been translated into English at least eleven times between 1893 and 1981. (See relevant bibliographies above and E.Yarwood "A Bibliography of Works by and about Vsevolod M.Garshin (1855-1888)", *Russian Literature Triquarterly*, 17 (1982), 230-1, 241.

* * * * *

"CHILDREN OF THE SUN"

A DRAMA OF UNPLACED SYMPATHIES

Cynthia Marsh

University of Nottingham,

England

Children of the Sun is perhaps the most neglected of all Gorky's plays not only in English but also in Soviet literary research. English translations of it have been scarce, productions are rare and there has been almost no critical writing about it./1/ While the work has always been readily available to Russians, Gorky's retrospective branding of it as a failure/2/ and its problematic structure have been responsible for its relatively minor place in the voluminous published material about Gorky.

This play caused problems from the very beginning. It was created in sensational circumstances, banned, claimed by two prominent theatres and caused a near-riot at its première in Moscow. Moreover, as more than one commentator has suggested,/3/ it not only caused a rift between Gorky and the Moscow Art Theatre (MAT),/4/ but also marked an important stage in the growth of the Theatre itself. It is these circumstances which have attracted critical attention rather than examination of the work itself as drama. The background to the writing of the play as well as its historical context will be briefly outlined first since much Soviet criticism depends upon them.

*   *   *   *

CYNTHIA MARSH

Gorky wrote the first version of *Children of the Sun* while incarcerated in the Peter and Paul Fortress in Petersburg in January and February, 1905. He had been arrested in the aftermath of Bloody Sunday. A few days later a request from his wife that he be allowed writing materials was granted, and having asked permission of the prison authorities to write a "comedy", Gorky drafted the first version between 5th and 14th February. On his release, facilitated largely by angry world opinion, he urged contacts to retrieve the play from the Police Department to which it had been submitted as required. Gorky recovered his play while in Riga, read it to his friends and intended finishing it off, although by then he was already working on his next play *The Barbarians* (VII,650).

Press announcements declared that the play would be given its première in Komissarzhevskaia's/5/ theatre in April. Gorky's first two successes had been with MAT - *The Lower Depths* and *Philistines*, both in 1902 - but the directors, or more particularly Nemirovich-Danchenko, had criticised his third play *Summerfolk* (1904), and a rift had developed in the partnership. Komissarzhevskaia's theatre had scored notably with it the previous autumn as one of its first productions. Greatly alarmed at the possibility of another Gorky première in Petersburg in the restless spring of 1905, the Governor-General successfully prevented the play from being performed in April. Thus Komissarzhevskaia was denied an early theatrical coup. The enforced delay allowed Gorky to polish the play./6/ He was also persuaded by his actress-mistress, a member of MAT,/7/ that she had been promised a role, and after an appeal by a galaxy of MAT actors including Kachalov/8/ and Stanislavsky, Gorky gave them equal performance rights. Thus MAT

CHILDREN OF THE SUN

secured its third but final and, for them, crucial play by Gorky.

In Finland that summer Gorky read his finished version of the play to a group of friends including Repin who left a sketch recording the occasion./9/ Also present was Kuprin whose comments were subsequently published in a newspaper article./10/ He remarked that the play had caused considerable argument, and that not because Gorky had been tendentious. The sincerity and vitality with which it was written had particularly attracted Kuprin. The play was premièred by both theatres in the two capitals in October. It was shepherded through the censorship in September, largely by Gorky's colleague Piatnitsky/11/ and by a letter from Gorky himself referring none too subtly to possible outraged European opinion should the play be banned (VII,655).

Even after MAT's intensive rehearsal schedule, Gorky was dissatisfied with the production and the première was postponed from 5th until 17th October, so Komissarzhevskaia was able to retrieve something of her intended coup by staging her première on October 12th in Petersburg. It was the Moscow première, however, which was sensational. The city's streets were restless as forces for both the left and right urged their points of view. Gorky's radical reputation ensured rumours of disruption at the first night. In the final act a malevolent crowd, terrified by a rising cholera epidemic, confronts the main character and blames him for the misfortune. When this crowd burst on to the stage with all the assiduous and authentic naturalism of the Art Theatre style, the audience panicked, believing a Moscow street riot had infiltrated the theatre. As required by his role, their favourite actor Kachalov fainted and many thought he had been shot. There was confusion. In an ironic reversal of roles the actors gaped at

CYNTHIA MARSH

the auditorium and the curtain was brought down on the audience, some of whom were scrambling for the exits, others shouting for Kachalov and yet others roaring their approval of the disorder. Nemirovich-Danchenko had to make a public announcement to calm the audience and the performance was restored only after a considerable delay. Many of those who had left did not return./12/ The scandal was fully reported in the newspapers the next day, confirming the play as another of Gorky's politically explosive works, though this in fact is a misleading judgment on *Children of the Sun*.

Gorky, however, in the growing revolutionary intensity of the weeks in October, had lost interest in his play. He was cynically amazed to find the actors still in rehearsal when they were surrounded by events of great social and political implication. He disliked the MAT production, preferring the Komissarzhevskaia version, though his mind was far from the theatre anyway (VII,656). His next two plays were banned by the censorship/13/ and the Gorky-MAT partnership came to an end. Some of the Theatre's members felt that with the deteriorating situation outside they should not be "play-acting" at all, and although *Children of the Sun* was performed twenty-one times between October and December, 1905, audiences dwindled as revolutionary events overtook Russia./14/ Early in the new year the Moscow Art Theatre went abroad for its first foreign tour and lost touch with Gorky, though they continued to give highly acclaimed performances of his two earlier plays./15/

*   *   *   *

Children of the Sun is set in the cholera epidemics of the early 1890s. Protasov is a young experimental scientist totally absorbed in his work

CHILDREN OF THE SUN

attempting to discover the secrets of matter and the beginning of life. He believes in the ability of science to improve the human condition. His devotion to his work blinds him to the needs of those around him and to the harsh reality of social conditions, seen here in the local disturbances due to a cholera epidemic. His entourage consists of his wife Elena whom he neglects in his absorption in his experiments, her admirer, the poet and artist Vagin, who matches Protasov's belief in science with an equally vital one in art, Protasov's neurotic sister Liza whose experience of a bloody brawl has left her in fear of the ordinary man in the street, and Liza's admirer, the local vet Chepurnoy, a cynical observer of the inadequacies of mankind. Other characters include Melaniia, the vet's widowed sister, the indispensable family nanny of this period (Antonovna), sundry servants, the odd-job man Egor, and Troshchin, a visiting acquaintance of Egor.

There is hardly a plot, rather a series of incidents which brings the characters together to expound their ideas in a Chekhovian manner. However, in Gorky they go on to express the chasms of political consciousness between them. For these intellectuals the conquering of darkness and ignorance is symbolised by the sun, the image which fathers them in the play's title. In their debate they compose a picture of heroic figures standing at the helm of a ship which they are steering towards the sun. For Protasov and Vagin the figures are the pioneers of science and art, while for Elena they are proud human beings ready to undertake any sacrifice even when they have to pass beneath the glaring sun of the desert. For Liza, however, the sand of Elena's desert is already symbolically blood-red and the voyage too late.

CYNTHIA MARSH

Elena is assiduously courted by Vagin, and Protasov is idolised by Chepurnoy's sister Melaniia to the extent that she offers him her fortune to continue his scientific work. Liza refuses Chepurnoy's offer of marriage, which drives him to suicide and then Liza to madness. Meanwhile rumours of Protasov's experiments are rife, and Egor, a formerly loyal helper who in common with most other peasants beats his wife and drinks heavily, loses her in the cholera epidemic. Together with his friend Troshchin, possibly a professional agitator, Egor heads a rabble in drunken pursuit of the local doctor to Protasov's house, determined to destroy him and his "medicines". Protasov is unable to understand Egor's hostility and insolence, nor why he should be regarded as the victim. With a revolver Elena halts the advancing crowd, which is then belaboured and forcibly dispersed by a henchman with a large piece of wood. Liza, having learnt of Chepurnoy's suicide, plays her final scene Ophelia-like in her madness, and Vagin closes the play with his verse comment on the hard lot of the intelligentsia.

*   *   *   *

The first two city premières differed significantly and foreshadowed future debates about the play. Komissarzhevskaia's Petersburg production presented the play as a satire on the inadequacies of the intelligentsia. They were mocked as effete, ineffectual and out of touch with the realities of everyday life./16/ The Moscow Art Theatre, on the other hand, caught the heroic potential of the main characters: the production emphasised their ability to build the future, even if this particular group seems sure to fail. As Durylin points out, they were in fact capitalising

CHILDREN OF THE SUN

on their experience of performing Chekhov. They played up the obduracy and ignorance of the "people" in the ugly scene with the crowd./17/ No wonder, he comments, the intelligentsia in the audience rose in fear at their presence! In the subsequent Soviet debate on this work, those with expectations of Gorky as a mouthpiece of the people see the play as undermining the position of the intelligentsia, showing how they have failed to accomplish the task set them, and revealing their subsequent "dangerous" alienation from the masses. For them Protasov is a weak, absent-minded scientist filled with misguided illusions, who has chosen his ivory tower and is indifferent to the fate of his wife, his sister and the people who serve him./18/ On the other hand, those who examine the play more closely and take into account the potentials of performance, discover a series of sympathetically-drawn characters. They are seen to be quite distinct from the negative portraits of the "bourgeois" intelligentsia in *Summerfolk*, *The Barbarians* and *Enemies*, the plays which stand closest to *Children of the Sun* in time and theme./19/ Protasov becomes a hero devoting himself body and soul to the cause of science in order to improve the lot of humanity; his neglect of those around him becomes excusable because of the depth of his concentration on his work. Nevertheless, he does have one inexcusable fault in Soviet terms: his neglect of the "people" and his failure to understand their position of hardship at the end of the play. Thus both Soviet interpretations suggest the production should end by condemning the hero, though to differing degrees.

Both interpretations leave some points to be explained: why, for example, is the play set in 1892/3? Why are there no positive representatives of the "people", but only the ignorant and obdurate instead? Why is there no strong voice heard from the revolutionary intelligentsia? The explanations and apologies for Gorky vary: the play must be produced in the "spirit" of Gorky, argue Durylin and Iuzovsky./20/ The "right" of the people and the "wrong" of the intelligentsia emerge by implication through the details of the comfortable life-style of the latter and the hardship and suffering of the former, declares Mikhailovsky;/21/ Egor and the people's role must be strongly projected, argues Iuzovsky again;/22/ 1905 intensified Gorky's hatred for the intelligentsia, and by returning to an earlier period, he wished to show when their moral bankruptcy had begun, Bialik decides./23/

These questions and explanations suggest a lack of ideological clarity in the text. In *Children of the Sun* Gorky had apparently left the audience in an uncertain position. Instead of reeling under the shock of his message, they were actually debating what the play was about. The play was, and has been, condemned as a failure by the ideological left because at best it found its audience uncommitted and at worst offered the possibility of approval by the right. However, its ambiguity has meant, too, that the ideological right and the centre have disregarded this work. It does not possess the clear ideological guidelines of Gorky's other plays, and in its relative obscurity it seems different, uncharacteristic of Gorky, and has therefore been regarded as a failure. If *Children of the Sun* is seen in the context of the plays Gorky had already written or was in the process of writing, then in terms of traditional literary criticism his drama stands clearly in the naturalistic school on the threshold of ideological theatre and represents certain views held by the author. In *Philistines* (1902), for example, Gorky had asked his audience to condemn

CHILDREN OF THE SUN

the bourgeoisie; in *The Lower Depths* (1902) he had confronted a surprised public with the dregs of the doss house; in *Summerfolk* (1904) sharp criticism of the intelligentsia is voiced by one of their own kind; *Barbarians* (1905) demonstrated the unacceptable and untenable position of an alienated intelligentsia in the face of the certain future of the "people"; and in *Enemies* (1906) the negative fate of the intelligentsia was uncompromisingly sealed. Without the closer investigation which has been denied this play, the ideological centre and right had little reason not to ignore it.

*   *   *   *

Exploration of *Children of the Sun* may not only discover the reasons for its neglect, but also reveal the nature of ideologically committed drama even if, ironically, by default. If the criterion of a "successful" Gorky play has been ideological commitment to the left, then how does *Children of the Sun* fail? What elements essential to ideological success had Gorky omitted or moderated? Had the usual dramatic channels for moulding audience response failed? Could his ideology be subverted by the text? In other words, was it the case that he had not sufficiently "placed" his sympathies? Discussion of differences from other contemporary plays by Gorky, of the lack of distinction made in this play between ideological hero and ideological villain, and of the capacity of the text to raise various audience responses, will provide some answers to these questions.

Soviet critics have pointed out a number of differences from the other Gorky plays of this period. The characters, for example, fall into a pattern which is distinct. Bialik points out that Gorky drops the ensemble mode in which there is a range of characters of roughly comparable weight, in favour of one central figure. For this reason and because of the change of setting from contemporary to historical, Bialik relegates the play to a quite separate category, treating it with two other less successful works, *Queer Folk* (1910) and the unfinished *Bogomolov* (1910)./24/ This relegation enhances the unsuccessful reputation of the play and allows what may be ideologically inconvenient to be explained as failure. Another difference suggested by Durylin among others/25/ is that the work's range of characters is far more limited than elsewhere. All the characters with speaking parts, that is excluding the crowd, can be defended as sympathetic, and the intelligentsia all assimilate to one type: they are all idealists and none has the negative bourgeois characteristics of *Summerfolk*, for example./26/ Nor are there any representatives of the newly-outspoken and self-critical intelligentsia heroes created by Gorky to make his social points. In other words, the wicked and easily condemnable here are not the intelligentsia. Gorky's ideological point, then, in this play is not clearly made.

The search for villains has led to some interesting Soviet interpretations of various secondary characters. There are those who attack Vagin as a representative of the "art for art's sake" group in the intelligentsia, a self-satisfied man who is frittering his life away in useless debate and unsuccessful amorous pursuits./27/ Occasionally he is defended for his devotion to art and for his care of the neglected Elena;/28/ Chepurnoy's cynicism is unpalatable to most, and yet, it could be argued, he is serving society as a vet, and is redeemed by his suffering which ends in suicide. Elena and Liza are almost universally praised for their awareness of the role of the "people" for Russia. Elena draws sympathetic

CHILDREN OF THE SUN

treatment for her husband's neglect of her, and only rare condemnation for her inclinations towards Vagin. Liza's premonitions of the bloodshed to come draw clear Soviet support, as does her rejection of the condescending attitudes of her brother and Vagin toward her views.

The unfortunate nature of the representatives of the masses is also explained from the ideological point of view./29/ Some critics have correctly perceived that if the people's voice falls to Egor, to Antonovna, the nanny, to Troshchin or to the panic-stricken rabble, they are forced to make their ideological point in a negative way, by default as it were. The audience has to be positively disposed to what is neither physically, intellectually, nor emotionally attractive./30/ A consideration of the network of potential relationships set up between this text in performance and its audience will illustrate the difficulty of these demands.

The naturalistic theatre in which Gorky's drama is located is a theatre of illusion. The audience is asked to suspend its disbelief in accepting for real what is patently artificial. Audience judgment is also coloured by the structuring of the play: the dramatist sets up his heroes to generate sympathy, and his villains, hostility. Ideological plays such as those by Gorky which fed on the realism of this kind of theatre, still depended on its current structure and style. Gorky's social ideology, however, was aimed precisely at those who produced and watched the naturalistic theatre of his day. He was both using the theatre and subverting it at the same time. He took his play structure from the existing convention, but his ideology presupposed that he had to portray as villains those whom the audience were expecting to regard as heroes.

In contrast to the clear-cut ideologies of *Philistines, The Lower*

CYNTHIA MARSH

Depths and *Summerfolk*, *Children of the Sun* fails to be tendentious. Instead of a deliberate generation of sympathy or hostility towards certain key characters, this play has at its heart a visually attractive symbolic system; it is a configuration of sun, sea, ships, helms and light over darkness, all symbolising heroism, adventure, endeavour and sacrifice It is only marginally moderated by Elena's glaring sun or Liza's red sand. Poetry is used to express the dilemma of these attractive heroes and heroines. Far from rebuffing the audience, the poetry reinforces the lyrical and heroic atmosphere. The ideological voice is only heard loud and clear in the violent and visually repulsive scene of confrontation at the end of the play, and is then lost in the spectacle of a young girl's madness. Where the ideological impact might be expected to be enhanced, the text is open to interpretation in performance. Questioning by various characters about the exclusion of such people as Egor or Antonovna from joining the ship in search of knowledge can give a humorous rather than an ideological twist to the material. For example, Soviet critics make much of the following exchange between Protasov and Egor near the beginning of the play. Urged on by the nanny and his sister, Protasov is reluctantly confronting Egor with the fact that the latter beats his wife.

Protasov: ...You are a man, a rational being, the brightest and finest thing on earth...
Egor (grinning): Who, me?
Protasov: Why, of course!

This conversation, urges Iuzovsky for example, sets the whole theme of the play as the increasingly unbridgeable gap between the intelligentsia and the "people"./31/ Protasov's reply demonstrates the unplumbable depths of his non-comprehension of real people. How can Protasov, they argue, make such a statement about tipsy, wife-beating Egor who is on the scrounge for

CHILDREN OF THE SUN

a rouble? He is simply incapable of perceiving the true situation. However, it is arguable that the text itself is open to humorous interpretation at this point. It is important to remember, as Iuzovsky fails to, that this exchange takes place in Act I before the audience has heard Protasov's eloquence on his own work and well before the presentation of his ideals in the high-flown speeches of Act II. The text allows for Egor to be the butt of the exchange as well as Protasov. Egor could knowingly accept the jibe as humorous and direct his "Who, me?" at the audience. Then an ironic smile from Protasov can be seen as his weary acknowledgment of the impossibility of reforming Egor.

Similarly, Mikhailovsky chooses to see Antonovna, the nanny, as a major figure, reading her opening lines where she fusses over Protasov as the key to the whole play./32/ He is correct in one respect, though: Antonovna's conversational exchanges are important but not so much for theme as for setting and story line. She functions as chorus, as a source of information, rather than as a figure designed to evoke the sympathies of the audience. Whilst fussing she manages to inform the audience about Egor, the cholera, Protasov's neglect of his wife, and Liza's delicate health, and she gives a hint that Protasov may have mortgaged his house to finance his work.

Performance style is an important issue here. In the more subtle part of his analysis Iuzovsky argues that only by creating a sympathetic performance style for Protasov can his ideological mistakes be perceived./33/ Then the audience will comprehend the two meanings implied in the play's title: on the one hand a serious devotion to science and capacity for self-sacrifice, on the other the irony of the "children" keeping the sun to themselves and refusing to acknowledge the darkness and ignorance about them. Is Iuzovsky not proposing, however, a theatrically difficult, if not impossible, task? Such a performance style would create sympathy between character and audience which must then be negated, if a critical stance is finally to be adopted. Similarly, Durylin argues, somewhat unconvincingly, that though the main characters may be perceived by the audience in a positive light, there must be no doubt that the heroes are misguided and should be condemned. To this end the play must be produced in the "spirit" of Gorky./34/ Iuzovsky goes so far as to conclude that if the text subverts the apparent ideological purpose, it must be corrected in performance./35/

What, then, has Gorky used in his play which creates sympathy between the audience and Protasov? He is indubitably the central character: most of the other characters are present by virtue of their relationship to him. They all have positive feelings for him (to varying degrees admittedly), but they act as channels of audience attention and attraction. Elena may suffer from his neglect, but her inability to make a break and go with Vagin suggests she still loves him. Liza, his sister, is still caught in admiration of his ideals and eloquence. Her perception of the chasm between intelligentsia and "people" is subverted by her madness. Her tragic end denies sympathy for her ideas, since they seem to be instrumental in her breakdown.

Vagin, though Protasov's rival in love and aesthetic beliefs, nevertheless shares his devotion to ideals and his lack of interest in everyday life, and moreover, supports his exclusive view of the intelligentsia. Antonovna, while she may disapprove of his behaviour, is devoted to

CHILDREN OF THE SUN

Protasov. For his part, Egor respects the man and willingly proffers his skills to ensure the work proceeds smoothly. Only Chepurnoy stands apart and could create a critical stance. His view of Protasov, however, is negated by his own failure in love and life. The conclusion is that no character who counts on sufficient sympathy to affect audience response, provides a constantly critical view of Protasov. The potential to do so could lie with Elena. She at least sees the gap between her husband and the broad mass of the people. But unlike some of Gorky's more vigorous heroines, she is incapable of unravelling her emotions and acting positively. It is also possible in performance that her relations with Vagin may generate a negative audience reaction to her. Its extent is directly proportional to the sympathy set up for Protasov.

It seems, therefore, that the "flaw", if it be such, in Gorky's play is his failure to incorporate a positive discrimination factor to favour those designed to speak out against the intelligentsia figures, a failure to "place" his ideological sympathies with certain characters. Such an omission can be partly excused on sociological and historical grounds as it is by some Soviet critics. In 1892 the individuals among the masses who were sufficiently politically conscious to stand on a par with the proletariat were very few. But, as Bialik points out, although Egor was a *remeslennik* (artisan) and not a *proletarii* (proletarian), the voice of the suffering "people" is still heard in his references to his hard lot./36/ What he does not ask, though, is why there is no other voice from the intelligentsia strong enough to make the relevant criticisms. The answer may lie in another comment by Bialik about Gorky's choice of the year 1892. Was he returning to a period when he thought the intelligentsia could possibly

119

have retrieved their position? Could they in fact have taken action to avoid the inevitable confrontation in the class struggle? If so, this would suggest a degree of sympathy with the intelligentsia that is unprecedented in Gorky's earlier or immediately subsequent works.

A comment made by Gorky to a Viennese newspaper after a production of *Children of the Sun* at the Berlin Kleines Theater of Max Reinhardt in March, 1906 shows that some of the idealism expressed by Protasov and Vagin also clung to Gorky. He hoped the gap between the intelligentsia and "people" was bridgeable. It was, he felt, the responsibility of those such as he who had struggled to attain knowledge, to make that knowledge a "beauty" accessible to all (VII,660). If this statement is viewed in sociological terms and particularly in Gorky's sociological terms, it is clear he was referring not to the intelligentsia of *Children of the Sun*, but to his own view of the new intelligentsia: the sons of former tradesmen, laundrymen and peasants who had fought for an education but who had not forgotten their social roots and were still ready to help the less fortunate. They are described by Maria Lvovna in *Summerfolk*./37/

Might we then consider *Children of the Sun* a kind of tragic elegy? Can it be regarded as an eloquent statement of regret that the intelligentsia, of whose values based on beauty and truth Gorky instinctively approved, had failed to capitalise on the moment when they could have closed the gap between themselves and the masses? Durylin argues that this interpretation arose from MAT's experience and success in playing Chekhov and inevitably produced a performance very different from Komissarzhevskaia's satire of the intelligentsia./38/ The arguments mountable against this interpretation of the play are strong in Soviet terms, however: the MAT production

CHILDREN OF THE SUN

was not a true reflection of the Gorky play, and it only demonstrated the company's lack of political consciousness, seen equally in their response to the events of autumn, 1905./39/ Others argue that the events of January, 1905 immediately preceding the creation of this play only served to intensify Gorky's hatred for the Tsarist regime and the Russian intelligentsia. The play must be seen in the light of the censorship, of current events and as a reflection of the insipid role of the intelligentsia in the events of Bloody Sunday. This remark from Gorky's letter to his wife E.P.Peshkova written shortly before his arrest on January 9th is frequently quoted:

> The first day of the Russian revolution was the day of the moral disgrace of the Russian intelligentsia./40/

Another frequently repeated piece of evidence as to the play's contemporary reference concerns Lebedev, a Moscow University professor of 1905, on whom Gorky is said to have modelled Protasov, and Kachalov to have based his stage interpretation./41/ Soviet critics, therefore, seem united against a tragic, elegaic interpretation of the work.

*   *   *   *

Another writer who figures in Soviet accounts of the background to the play is Leonid Andreev. In one sense he supports the view that the play was an outspoken social criticism of the intelligentsia, while in another he indicates other facts which may have had an influence on its genesis. The history of the association between Gorky and Andreev is well-documented and need not be given in great detail here./42/ Their friendship dated from the 1890s, and in 1903 they entertained the idea of collaborating on a play. Both had been intrigued by the Russian translation of a book by a German writer, Herman Klein, printed by the "Znanie" publishing house in 1900./43/ References in their correspondence suggest that the idea for a play in response to the book took root in 1903./44/ Andreev recorded his idea enthusiastically. He was struck by the polarisation of the following vision: an astronomer living on top of a hill has his view entirely concentrated on the stars with no thought for affairs on earth. Meanwhile, down below him a revolution is taking place, the people quite oblivious of the heavens above. In October, 1903 Gorky wrote of possible collaboration to Piatnitsky./45/ By the spring of 1904 Gorky was writing to Andreev to ask if he could take over the astronomer theme for himself,/46/ but in May Andreev responded that he would not give it up under any circumstances, and that he had already progressed some way with the project. He was, therefore, still thinking in terms of a collaboration./47/ After that there was some cooling off in their relationship, and Gorky clearly felt the subject was his when he finally put pen to paper in prison the following February. The play was conceived by Andreev and Gorky to unmask the "ivory tower" scientist. In both their letters there are references to delight at seeing the intellectual receiving his just deserts *vis-à-vis* the people, the *tolpa* (crowd), as Gorky put it./48/ The disapproval that such a play would call forth from the middle-class audience was relished by both men. Andreev verbally caricatures Gorky and himself as authors receiving an ovation of rotten eggs, bad oranges and flying boots./47/ Yet, on the other hand, as pointed out in the 1970 collected edition of Gorky's works (VII,647), Klein's book contains references to the "children of the sun", a phrase that was to give Gorky his

CHILDREN OF THE SUN

title. Works of genius in the arts and sciences, Klein argues, are a reflection of the sun, as a symbol of life and knowledge. Sun symbolism achieved its own vogue in Russia at the turn of the century in the work of the rising generation of Symbolists. Bal'mont's call in chorus with other Symbolist poets "Let us be like the sun!", reflected a desire for other worlds and ecstatic experience which found a warm response among the burgeoning modernist intelligentsia of the day./50/ Gorky was attracted to the imagery but had perhaps hoped to append a different ideology to it. Was he caught between his attraction to the symbolism, his love of ideals and florid imagery on the one hand, and his desire to write a socially critical play on the other?

*   *   *   *

The conclusion seems to be that to make an ideological point in the context of naturalistic drama requires the kind of positive discrimination which is at odds with the nature of the material being presented. It is conceivable that Gorky in his fight to give the masses a voice, may have felt that such a line of action was totally justifiable. But on this occasion he was perhaps "led astray" by the social reality of the historical period he was presenting, and by his attraction to ideals and to an eloquent means for their expression.

Various Soviet critics argue that Gorky's voice is one of the few reflecting the true socio-political picture of the first Russian revolution of 1905. However, the note of elegy, of regret even, for the lost role of the intelligentsia that can sound in *Children of the Sun* in performance was as much a part of that pattern of socio-political developments, and

CYNTHIA MARSH

Gorky was being honest with himself and his society in echoing it. His play should be allowed to stand on its own merits as a text for performance and not be neglected or explained away as ideologically biased or inconvenient as has so often been the case. The refusal of this text to be compartmentalised and ideologically "correct" stems from the complexity of the year when it was composed: 1905. Moreover, an examination of the text's potential in performance suggests that it is far less ideologically committed than has generally been thought. And despite that fact, or even because of it (depending on which side of the ideological fence one sits), Gorky's *Children of the Sun* is an eminently performable play.

NOTES
1. M.Gorky, *The Children of the Sun*, tr. M.Budberg (London, 1973). This is the only recent translation located; two others date from 1906 and 1912. G.M.Terry's *Maxim Gorky in English: A Bibliography 1868-1936-1986* (Nottingham, 1986) cites no works of direct reference in English. H.Segel, "Gorky's Major Plays", *Yale Theatre*, 7/2 (1976), 56-77; his *Twentieth Century Russian Drama: From Gorky to the Present* (New York, 1979); and F.M.Borras, *Maxim Gorky the Writer* (Oxford, 1967), do not mention it.
2. *Polnoe sobranie sochinenii: khudozhestvennye proizvedeniia v dvadtsati piati tomakh* (Moscow, 1970), Vol.7, p.661. Gorky referred to the play as *neudachnaia* (unsuccessful) in his notes to the story "The Watchman" published in 1922-23 (*PSS*: XV,81). The notes on *Children of the Sun* in the 1970 edition are far fuller than in the 1949-53 edition. There seems to have been a reluctance to explore the play too deeply as its insecure ideological position presented difficulties. Reference in this article is to the 1970 edition (hereinafter incorporated in the text), and except where otherwise stated, much of the background material is taken from this source.
3. See, for example, S.Durylin, "Gor'kii na tsene", in *Gor'kii i teatr: sbornik statei* (Moscow-Leningrad, 1938), p.246, and V.I.Nemirovich-Danchenko, *My Life in the Russian Theatre*, tr. J.Cournos (London, 1937), p.268. When available, English translations of Russian sources have been quoted in this article.
4. The Moscow Art Theatre was founded by K.S.Stanislavsky and V.I.Nemirovich-Danchenko in 1898. Major sources of information on the Theatre and its links with Gorky are to be found in the autobiographies of the two

CHILDREN OF THE SUN

founders: K.Stanislavsky, *My Life in Art* (London, 1980) and V.I.Nemirovich-Danchenko, *op.cit*.
5. V.F.Komissarzhevskaia (1864-1910). She established her reputation as an actress in the Imperial theatres between 1896 and 1904. She then ran her own theatre between 1904 and 1907 in St. Petersburg, producing plays by contemporary dramatists such as Chekhov, Gorky and Ibsen. Later she moved on to writers of the Modernist movement, including Maeterlinck, Blok and Sologub.
6. See S.Balukhatyi, "Rabota M.Gor'kogo nad p'esoi *Deti solntsa*: materialy i nabliudeniia", in *M.Gor'kii: materialy i issledovaniia* (Leningrad, 1934), Vol.1, pp.459-505, for a study of the various manuscripts of the play.
7. M.F.Andreeva (1868-1953).
8. V.I.Kachalov (Shverubovich) (1875-1948). - An actor who joined MAT in 1900 and remained there until his death, during which time he played 55 different roles.
9. Repin's sketch has been reproduced in a number of sources, including I.S.Novich, *M.Gor'kii v epokhu pervoi russkoi revoliutsii* (Moscow, 1960), pp.144-5, and "Gor'kii i Leonid Andreev: neizdannaia perepiska", *Literaturnoe nasledstvo*, 72 (1965), 263 (henceforth cited as *Lit. nasledstvo 72*).
10. See *Odesskie novosti*, No.6691 (July 14, 1905); quoted in *PSS*: VII,652-3.
11. K.P.Piatnitskii (1864-1938). - A close associate of Gorky's from the "Znanie" publishing co-operative.
12. See Nemirovich-Danchenko, *op.cit.*, pp.261-3.
13. They were *Barbarians* (1905) and *Enemies* (1906).
14. See Nemirovich-Danchenko, *op.cit.*, p.265.
15. See, for example, J.Hunneker, *Iconoclasts: A Book of Dramatists* (London, 1906), pp.269-85.
16. See *PSS*: VII,656-7. Some hostile reviews are quoted by Durylin, *op cit.*, p.251.
17. See Durylin, *op.cit.*, pp.246-7.
18. See, for example, Novich, *op.cit.*, pp.144-5; and V.Novikov, *Tvorcheskaia laboratoriia Gor'kogo-dramaturga* (Moscow, 1965), p.465.
19. See, for example, B.Bialik, *M.Gor'kii - dramaturg* (Moscow, 1977), p.297; M.Grigor'ev, *Gor'kii: dramaturg i kritik* (Moscow, 1946), p.37; and B.V.Mikhailovskii, *Dramaturgiia M.Gor'kogo epokhi pervoi russkoi revoliutsii* (Moscow, 1955), p.153.
20. Durylin, *op.cit.*, p.247; Iu.Iuzovskii, "Tvorcheskie idei Gor'kogo", in *Gor'kii i teatr* (Moscow-Leningrad, 1938), p.77.
21. Mikhailovskii, *op.cit.*, p.190.
22. Iuzovskii, *op.cit.*, p.77.
23. Bialik, *op.cit.*, pp.295-6.
24. *Ibid.*, p.177.
25. Durylin, *op.cit.*, p.246.
26. See V.V.Mikhailovskii, "Tema intelligentsii v rannei dramaturgii Gor'kogo", in *Gor'kovskie chteniia 1949-50* (Moscow, 1951), pp.346-7.
27. Iuzovskii, *op.cit.*, pp.72-3; Novikov, *op.cit.*, p.464; Grigor'ev, *op cit.*, pp.41-2.
28. Mikhailovskii, "Tema", *op.cit.*, p.348.

29. Bialik, *op. cit.*, p.300, and Novich, *op. cit.*, pp.49-50.
30. Durylin, *op. cit.*, p.247.
31. Iuzovskii, *op. cit.*, p.72.
32. Mikhailovskii, *op. cit.*, p.187.
33. Iuzovskii, *op. cit.*, p.71.
34. Durylin, *op. cit.*, p.247.
35. Iuzovskii, *op. cit.*, p.77.
36. Bialik, *op. cit.*, p.300.
37. *PSS*: VII,269,278, and M.Gorky, *Five Plays* (Moscow, 195-), p.333.
38. Durylin, *op. cit.*, p.246.
39. *Ibid.*, p.247.
40. See, for example, Bialik, *op. cit.*, pp.295-6.
41. *Ibid.*, p.297, and Durylin, *op. cit.*, pp.246-7.
42. See, for example, *Lit. nasledstvo*, 72, and J.Woodward, *Leonid Andreyev* (Oxford, 1969).
43. G.Klein, *Astronomicheskie vechera* (St. Petersburg, 1900).
44. *Lit. nasledstvo*, 72, p.422.
45. *Ibid.*, p.211, n.2.
46. *Ibid.*, p.210.
47. *Ibid.*, p.113.
48. *Ibid.*, p.210.
49. *Ibid.*, p.113, letter 104.
50. K.D.Bal'mont, *Budem kak solntse* (Moscow, 1903). For a discussion of this symbol, see also L.Dolgopolov, "Vokrug 'detei solntsa'", in *M. Gor'kii i ego sovremenniki* (Leningrad, 1968), pp.79-109.

* * * * *

GORKY, NIETZSCHE AND GOD-BUILDING

Edith W. Clowes

Purdue University,

Indiana, U.S.A.

"Gorky and Nietzsche" has emerged as a significant topic in Gorky criticism of the last two decades. Perhaps it has won more notoriety than it deserves because Soviet critics have protested so vehemently against the possibility of the influence of a "decadent", "proto-Nazi" thinker upon a "realist", "radical" writer./1/ This claim, it is argued, is an attempt by "bourgeois" critics to denigrate the "father of Socialist Realism". However, only orthodox Soviet critics might deny this particular literary relationship. For a number of other commentators (from both socialist and capitalist countries), the topic has opened up a fresh approach to Gorky, bringing out complexities of his literary character that have long been overlooked./2/

While the standard Soviet interpretation shows the Russian writer and the German philosopher as irreconcilable enemies, the gradual publication of the Gorky archive and the appearance of the complete critical edition of his belletristic work have revealed a more productive relationship. In the English-speaking world a number of doctoral dissertations treat Nietzsche's work, particularly *Thus Spoke Zarathustra*, as a tremendous intellectual stimulant for the young Gorky./3/ In published form, George Kline first suggested that Nietzsche was an influence in the development of Gorky's world-view, and discussed from an intellectual-historical standpoint the parallels in their thinking./4/ Betty Forman has shown through close textual analysis that Gorky was reading and appropriating Nietzsche's thought from the early 1890s on./5/ More recently, Louise Loe has suggested the importance of Gorky's interpretation of Nietzsche for his formulation of the relationship between the intelligentsia and the Russian people./6/

Despite these studies, however, the full importance of the Gorky-Nietzsche relationship remains far from clear. It is often assumed that the active, creative period of appropriation ended in 1904-05 with the public failure of Gorky's "Man" (1904), a programmatic piece with a vision of future man broadly perceived as "Nietzschean", and Gorky's subsequent apparent detraction of Nietzsche in his "Notes on the *Meshchanstvo*" (1905). Raimund Sesterhenn has argued that in the following "God-building" period a more subtle appropriation process was at work./7/ It appears to me that during the years 1907-13 Gorky made the transition from an apprenticeship to Nietzsche to full and independent maturity. His early myths of human self-transformation in such works as "Reader" (1898) and "Man" can be seen as creative deformations of Nietzsche's myth of self-overcoming./8/ In these pieces Gorky openly admits the subtext through direct "quotation" of significant images and figures. But he arrives now at his own myth of regeneration. The maturation process comes about through an attitude of productive adversity. On the face of things Gorky appears to reject his mentor. A close look, though, shows that he switches identity with him, remaking Nietzsche in his own image whilst subtly claiming Nietzschean attitudes as his own and placing them in a wholly unfamiliar context where they lose their immediate link with the subtext.

GORKY, NIETZSCHE AND GOD-BUILDING

Perhaps Gorky himself gives the best clue to his adversarial attitude to significant precursors such as Nietzsche in his response to a poll on religious consciousness published in mid-1907 in the French journal *Mercure de France*. Precursors, he suggests here, must be mastered and overcome in the name of humanity's continued sense of dignity and its will to explore, develop and perfect itself. The human race, he claims, is about to witness the "conception of a new psychological type"./9/ This claim is not new, however, for it is as old as Prometheus and as recent as the superman. In his attitude to great precursors, Gorky certainly felt what Harold Bloom calls "belatedness" - that is, the fate of coming historically after a great epoch and living in its shadow./10/ However, like many other writers of his day, Gorky counterbalances and indeed overcomes that sense of belatedness with a much more pressing sense of what may be called "future anxiety". He competes with both predecessors and contemporaries to leave his imprint on future human consciousness, and insists on his right to exploit those predecessors and to shape his own model for the future. The advantage enjoyed by those living in the present over the powerful masters of the past, he writes, is their ability to synthesise, broaden and push human knowledge to new limits: they can "master" the masters. "The act of mastery", Gorky explains, "enriches a person and awakens in him the consciousness of his own worth - the commanding and proud desire to compete in creative activity (*tvorchestvo*) with past generations and to make models which are worthy of serving the future"./11/ Thus deep creativity - that is, the further perfection of human nature - is fostered by competing with and overcoming past "ideals". We find Gorky's "mastery" of his great German precursor in the God-building myth which informs two of his finest

EDITH W. CLOWES

prose works, *Confession* (1908) and *Childhood* (1913). Gorky's own process of "overcoming" his mentor took place in the highly-charged milieu of Russian radical political and literary activity of the early 1900s. Nietzsche's work was the focal point of debate at the time and, in a negative way, was a touchstone for so-called "right-thinking" among radicals. After the débâcle of the 1905 revolution, two of Gorky's closest associates in exile were Vladimir Lenin and Anatoly Lunacharsky. The first was wholly opposed to Nietzsche's work, the second as captivated by it as Gorky was. Through his 1905 article "Party Organisation and Party Literature", Lenin put pressure on socialist-oriented writers to develop a collectivist creative psychology. Indirectly he labelled Nietzsche as élitist and individualist when he used the phrase "literary supermen" pejoratively to mean esoteric writers or those who catered to educated "bourgeois" taste./12/ He described such artists as ineffectual and ultimately of little historical significance. In contrast, writers who joined forces with the people and the Party, he suggested, would share in a great historical mission and would have a hand in building future Russian society. In his "Notes on the *Meshchanstvo*" Gorky apparently responded to Lenin's lead by openly characterising Nietzsche as a "bourgeois" philosopher and by promoting a collectivist mentality./13/ However, Lenin's objections to Nietzsche did nothing substantial to alter Gorky's enthusiasm for his philosophical mentor. In fact, during these years Gorky had less to do with Lenin than with Lunacharsky, with whom he collaborated in the workers' school on Capri and in the publication of two anti-Modernist collections, *Literary Decline* (I-II, 1908-09) and *Sketches on the Philosophy of Collectivism* (1908). The two men shared the same interest in conceiving

GORKY, NIETZSCHE AND GOD-BUILDING

a socialist aesthetic, a vision of art and creativity that would play a central role in building the coming Utopia. Both writers also shared an enthusiasm for Nietzsche. Furthermore, Lunacharsky was an active supporter of the Nietzschean aspects of Gorky's art - something that was rare for a radical. As early as 1903, for example, he had openly linked the writer with a Nietzschean world-view./14/ Gorky's heroes, though proto-proletarians, were endowed with what Lunacharsky recognised as Nietzschean virtues: belligerence, egotism (albeit what Lunacharsky called "collective" egotism!), and monumental, world-transfiguring, creative genius.

In addition to his enthusiasm for Nietzsche, Lunacharsky's longstanding interest in the history of religion was to bolster Gorky's own search for a myth of social renewal. Lunacharsky had studied philosophy and religion abroad, and between 1908 and 1911 published the major work of his middle career, *Religion and Socialism*./15/ The God-building myth which he developed here rested, in part, on Nietzschean ideas. He argued for an anthropological approach to religion that went beyond Feuerbach's theory that God was a projection of the essence of human nature. The human psyche, Lunacharsky agreed with Nietzsche, was the only signifying power in existence./16/ Lunacharsky's myth was intended to do rather more than overcome the sense of alienation that Feuerbach saw in religion: it was meant as a response to Nietzsche's call to revalue existing values, to forge new and vital consciousness. For Lunacharsky, as for Nietzsche, the highest unconditional value is "life", and the goal of existence is to "maximalise" life./17/ Maximalisation Lunacharsky interpreted as meaning the achievement of "right-feeling" - again as with Nietzsche - a form of intoxication with existence that the Russian writer called "enthusiasm".

EDITH W. CLOWES

The new consciousness that Lunacharsky foresaw was collectivist, and here he differed from the German philosopher whom he so admired. The transformation of human nature, in his view, would come about when the highly-cultured but isolated and feckless self merged with the greater-than-human "we", the vital force of the masses.

In his search for human renewal during this period, Gorky felt a close affinity for Lunacharsky. Indeed, Lunacharsky's vision was to play an important role in Gorky's re-reading of Nietzsche and in his attempts to overcome this early mentor. Even after the débâcle of 1905, his sudden departure into exile and his increasingly close work with the Bolshevik Party, Gorky made Nietzsche's philosophy part of his public intellectual profile. While raising funds for the Russian Social Democrats in New York in 1906, for example, he invited discussion of his favourite writers, prominent among whom was Nietzsche./18/ In the same year word reached Nietzsche's sister that the Russian radical admired her brother's work, and she sent him an invitation to visit the philosopher's archive in Weimar./19/

A letter from Gorky to the writer L. A. Nikiforova in 1910 reveals the switch of identities that marked Gorky's move from apprentice to master. Here Gorky defends Nietzsche against his popular image as a crude individualist. As he puts it, Nietzsche was a "bad individualist" because he wanted too much for humanity./20/ Gorky then characterises his mentor in terms of his own emerging concept of *lichnost'* (selfhood), while treating originally Nietzschean ideas as his own. Nietzsche appears in this letter as a Gorkian type, full of anger at social injustice. In contrast, Gorky imbues his own ideal of the social self with a Nietzschean will to deep

GORKY, NIETZSCHE AND GOD-BUILDING

creativity, a will to "make new forms of life".

In his public treatment of his mentor Gorky exhibits the same pattern of switched identity but masked now by an apparently antagonistic attitude. In both "Notes on the *Meshchanstvo*" and a later article, "Destruction of the Self" (1909), he distances himself from Nietzsche by portraying the German as a "bourgeois" philosopher filled with a "hatred of democracy" (SS: XXIII,344; XXIV,44). However, this seeming hostility, it can be argued, is relatively superficial and is put there, at least in part, to satisfy the writer's radical readership. The class stereotyping draws attention away from Gorky's profound admiration for the German philosopher. He never actually calls Nietzsche "bourgeois", and he casts aspersions not directly on Nietzsche but on his passive, self-satisfied and stupid middle-class audience. Nietzsche himself, though, is painted in the most glowing of terms. Here again he is given the attributes of Gorkian heroes such as Danko in "The Old Woman Izergil" (1895). He has "new hot blood" and "fire" in his soul (SS: XXIII,345); he calls his readers to action, to quest and change (SS: XXIII,345; XXIV,44). It is hardly his fault that the educated bourgeois audience to whom Nietzsche addressed himself did not heed his call. By discrediting one audience and its interpretation, Gorky subtly leaves open the possibility for another, more active and potent appropriation. By showing that he is not one of the "literary supermen" whom Lenin derided - by dissociating himself from vulgar Nietzschean "individualism" - Gorky sets up the disguise for a collectivist re-evaluation of Nietzsche. He interpolates into his God-building myth material of Nietzschean origin, now well-laundered through his own earlier appropriations and through Lunacharsky's socialist-religious reading. The moral outlook created in Gorky's major fictional work of the period, his *Confession*, also leads the reader away from an association with Nietzsche. Gorky's moral consciousness here is collectivist in character and he preaches the ethic of pity that was so pervasively criticised by Nietzsche. Monied, cultured and powerful protagonists are undermined, while the lowly are treated as heroes. Thus Gorky covers the tracks left by his precursor and establishes his own characteristic themes, hero-types and codes of valuation. The God-building myth would be Gorky's declaration of independence from an extremely influential mentor. As such, it is a response to Nietzsche's perceived call for action, the call to improve, to overcome human nature as it exists and to know a "new greatness of man". And it is a Gorkian "revaluation of values". Henceforth, as Gorky alluded to Nietzschean issues, he would impose his own interpretation on them.

Gorky's God-building myth has much in common with Lunacharsky's in that here Lunacharsky's basic positions are dramatised and historicised. But Gorky pays more attention than Lunacharsky does to issues of creative genius and to the nature of mass creative consciousness. And, to a greater degree than Lunacharsky does, he tries to sketch the outlines of perfected human nature, of *lichnost'* in the future.

Underlying Gorky's collectivist myth we find an aesthetic vision that is close in many ways to Nietzsche's. In *Zarathustra* Nietzsche distinguishes between *Kunst* - craft, art, shaping power - and *Schöpfung* - deep, mythopoetic, evaluative creativity. He finds both faculties essential but gives greater weight to *Schöpfung*. Gorky, like his mentor, distinguishes between *iskusstvo* (art) and *tvorchestvo* (value-giving, creative drive). But there the comparison ends. If Nietzsche makes fun of contemporary art, he treats high culture in general as the greatest of human achievements.

GORKY, NIETZSCHE AND GOD-BUILDING

By contrast, Gorky in "On Cynicism" (1908) denigrates all high culture and its artistic forms (SS: XXIV,6). In "Destruction of the Self" he belittles the classic great works of art and their makers, things which Nietzsche had admired. Although both faculties represent profound, value-giving creativity, *Schöpfung* and *tvorchestvo* are treated in very different ways by each writer. *Schöpfung* is an inner psychic drive, while *tvorchestvo* is a will exerted only by the united masses of humanity. No single human being possesses it. As Gorky puts it in "Destruction of the Self": "Art (*iskusstvo*) is in the power of the individual, only the collective is capable of creation (*tvorchestvo*)" (SS: XXIV,34). While Nietzsche sees Apollonian *Kunst* as the finest product of the deeper Dionysian force, Gorky clearly values the life-giving surge of collective will and finds something comparatively insubstantial and weak in individual works of art. Here we find in Gorky a new expression of the Romantic *narodnost'* (nationalism) so prevalent in the critical theory of Belinsky and Grigorev: works of art are great only insofar as they convey national will.

In his *Confession* and *Childhood*, Gorky belittles finished artistic form in favour of spontaneous personal expression and mass ritual. For example, in *Childhood* the young Gorky cannot learn the classical Russian poems that his mother reads to him. The sounds in them seem absurd. By contrast, he can listen for hours to his grandmother's spontaneously fresh and beautiful prayers. In *Confession*, Matvei finds little satisfaction in canonised church ritual, but is transported first by the stories and philosophising of the wanderer, Iegudiil, and later by the great and spontaneous gatherings of workers. Gorky's objections to the idea of *iskusstvo* are reflected in the very structure of *Confession* and *Childhood*. He was well-known for his dissatisfaction with his own finished products, and it has frequently been argued that most of his longer works have serious structural flaws./21/ It seems no accident that two of his most successful works - those under discussion here - have spontaneity as their basic structural motif. Both are emotionally-charged, first-person narratives bound together by the character and the moral and spiritual searching of the narrator. The first is a "confession", and its dynamism stems from the speaker's intensely emotional attempt to reveal and perfect his nature. The second is an autobiography which similarly is a revelation of self, an emotional examination of personal history to find the roots of selfhood. In addition, both works thematically are concerned with self-overcoming through a mythic search for *tvorchestvo*, for vital creative will.

Tvorchestvo in Gorky's mythic structure is unleashed when the individual consciousness merges with the colossal energy of the masses (SS: XXIV, 5,34,79). The ego, Gorky agrees with Nietzsche, is at best an empty shadow unless it has preserved its vital tie with deeper life energy./22/ Nietzsche sees this energy source in the "body" (*Leib*), that is, the subconscious "self" (*Selbst*). Gorky, by contrast, sees the same Dionysian force in the social "body" of humanity. Thus the masses are analogous to Nietzsche's "self", while the creative, self-conscious individual can be compared to Nietzsche's "ego".

To Gorky the fusion of individual self-consciousness and collective creative energy is the only way to achieve self-transformation. In "On Cynicism" he makes the point that this life-giving union brings "great joy and thirst for the creation of new forms for new culture" (SS: XXIV,6). In *Confession* and *Childhood* two of his most vital characters exemplify the

GORKY, NIETZSCHE AND GOD-BUILDING

new consciousness. Thus the hero of *Confession*, Matvei, finds in the wanderer Iegudiil an invigorating spirit the like of which he has never met. The strength of Gorky's relationship with his former "master", Nietzsche, is confirmed in this pivotal character. Moreover, Gorky alludes closely to Nietzschean sources in *The Birth of Tragedy* and *Zarathustra*, though the traces are well-covered. Iegudiil resembles Zarathustra in the guise of a Russian sectarian. Like Zarathustra, he is irreverent and gay: both have played all the traditional roles of a holy man and have found them lacking. Iegudiil develops Gorky's ideas from the *Mercure de France* fragment that religious faith means growth, creativity and the expansion of horizons, not submission to ritualised action and thought. Speaking of religious faith, he virtually quotes Nietzsche's thoughts on tragedy in the 1886 preface to his *Birth of Tragedy* when he says that faith is "born of an excess of human life force" (IX,340). Iegudiil himself is filled with this overflowing energy and he speaks as if he were "drunk with joy" (IX,341). His rejection of traditional value systems has laid him open to the tremendous vitality of spontaneous, mass mythopoetic energy. The link with these blind, mythopoetic forces enables him to formulate new myth. He speaks in his own Church Slavonic idiom and he has the power to coin new words. It is he who first uses the word "God-building" (*bogostroitel'stvo*). The actual narrative of the myth realises the kind of synthetic "mastery" of the past that Gorky mentioned in *Mercure de France*. Iegudiil weaves elements from Feuerbach's religious anthropology, Marx's Prometheanism and Nietzsche's Dionysian myth into his own vision of the future. He pictures the masses as a Dionysian force which gives meaning to existence only to become alienated from the heroes and deities that it has itself created.

137

EDITH W. CLOWES

Divine power, which, as Iegudiil explains, was simply an intense concentration of collective will, appears to acquire a life and creative energy of its own. Society's leaders nurture an image of the divine as an independent, universal and dominative principle. Iegudiil believes that the masses are just reawaking from their torpor of submissiveness and will soon reassert their own God-like creative power (IX,342).

Gorky achieves a brilliantly convincing and unprogrammatic vision of God-building *tvorchestvo* in *Childhood* in the character of Grandmother Kashirina. Here the grandfather and grandmother with whom the young boy grows up are archetypes of two kinds of class consciousness. Grandfather Kashirin is the dogmatic, ungenerous petty bourgeois, while Grandmother Kashirina represents the masses, the people as a whole. Although each character views himself as a Christian, each "builds" his own vision of God as a kind of projection of his subconscious. Thus the grandmother's God reflects her own life-affirming joyfulness:

> Her God was with her all day, and she even talked about him to animals. It was plain that it was easy for everything to submit to this God: people, dogs, birds, bees, even herbs. He bestowed this kindness on all earthly creatures without distinction, and was close to all things (Ch: 101).

Much like Iegudiil, the grandmother's mythopoetic energy gives her the ability to find a unique mode of expression and to compose her own prayers.

The personalities of Gorky's two God-building protagonists share an extremely important element that links them with their Dionysian predecessor. The God-building myth is built on an androgynous idea and the personalities of both Iegudiil and Grandmother Kashirina combine elements of both sexes. Iegudiil is described as laughing "tenderly, like a woman" (IX,342), while Grandmother Kashirina has the expressive, artistic gift that Gorky usually

GORKY, NIETZSCHE AND GOD-BUILDING

associates with male characters. Furthermore, her image of divinity is as likely to be female as male, for she prays to God as the Virgin Mary or the Queen of Heaven just as frequently as she does to the Father. In emphasising this male/female unity, Gorky underscores the idea of entire human unity which forms the basis of his new myth.

God-building types such as Iegudiil and Grandmother Kashirina represent the psychological condition through which human nature will escape from its present oppressed state. They help to foster mythopoetry. But they are not the end goal of transfigured human consciousness, for each still lives too much as an outsider *vis-à-vis* the old, oppressive mythic code. In his "Destruction of Selfhood" Gorky best anticipates the new human *lichnost'* which will eventually emerge. It will be in the form of a greater-than-human archetypal leader who embodies the aspirations of the entire people. As an example of such an archetype created through a broad national movement, he uses Faust. As he puts it: "In such times of social upheaval [as the German Reformation], the *lichnost'* becomes a focal point for thousands of wills which have chosen it as its voice, and it arises before us in the wonderful light of beauty and strength, in the bright flame of the desires of its people" (SS: XXIV,34). Here again we find a certain analogy with Nietzsche's aesthetic view, but there is also an essential difference. In his *Birth of Tragedy* Nietzsche argues that the Apollonian hero appears as a concrete, if transient, embodiment of the Dionysian will. Now Gorky fuses this idea with the Romantic notion that great art expresses the essence of national will. To him national will has acquired Dionysian qualities of rebelliousness and creativity. Not only that, but national will, as Gorky sees it, is no fixed phenomenon: instead, it evolves over time, cyclically conceiving new myth, and with it, new goals, values and heroes.

Although Gorky's belletristic work is full of a messianic anticipation of future *lichnost'*, it does not actually produce a mythic archetype. His protagonists, Matvei and he himself as a young boy, cannot be seen as such. They are at most witnesses to the rumblings and murmurings of awakening mass consciousness. Here real questions arise as to whether Gorky successfully answered Nietzsche's call to create new myth and achieved his goal of mastering the "masters" of the past: the moral and aesthetic consciousness underlying Gorky's God-building attempt is both problematic and difficult. While he seems to wish to foster fresh creativity, he largely reaffirms traditional socialist and Populist positions, something which Nietzsche would have seen as "herd" mentality. Although Gorky champions the monumental creative genius of the masses, he is at a loss to let it demonstrate itself.

Gorky's God-building reveals a radical apocalyptic mentality. He is intent on tearing down the value structures of the present which, he argues, are decadent. Nothing of the present should be salvaged, and high art with its moribund forms must give way to the brute, mythopoetic sweep of mass consciousness. The refined self-reflection of high culture and the contrived ratiocination of individual self-consciousness must be replaced by "enthusiasm". All this is very well, but when Gorky shows the masses in action, we find no trace of creative drive. At the end of *Confession*, for example, Matvei attends a kind of faith-healing demonstration during which a cripple regains the ability to walk. The feeling which grips and unites everyone present is pity (*zhalost'*), and though this emotion has a kind of

GORKY, NIETZSCHE AND GOD-BUILDING

healing power, it does not manifest mythopoetic energy. Gorky has merely put the masses in place of Christ. At most, this scene is a sentimental re-enactment of an incomparably more powerful New Testament episode. The question arises as to whether Gorky is merely refashioning old myths and the ethical codes that 19th century socialists and Populists heralded. If so, then the God-building myth as such has failed. However, God-building remains a powerful principle if we understand it as a dream of human nobility conceived by Iegudiil and embodied in Grandmother Kashirina, a dream which inspires the two narrators who are in search of themselves. In their moral self-sufficiency and imaginative energy these characters rank among the finest in Russian literature. Here Gorky has remained true to himself: he has created his own mythic archetype which in no way imitates archetypes that he clearly admires: Prometheus, Faust and the superman. Perhaps his "failure" to produce a superhuman hero is really no failure at all, but a way of mastering the experience of the past. Perfection achieved becomes oppressive. Feuerbach pointed out the ruinous alienation present in the relationship between imperfect man and perfect deity, while Dostoevsky asserted that humanity loves to strive for perfection but never to attain it. Iegudiil realises the danger inherent in "images of perfection": they are "made hastily" and bring "harm and misery" (IX,341). Thus in *Confession* and *Childhood*, Gorky upholds the idea of spontaneity, growth and creative inventiveness. He champions the human principle of *tvorchestvo* over any one superhuman product.

Both *Confession* and *Childhood* won praise even from the author's most adamant critics for their literary mastery and philosophical maturity. In his review of *Childhood*, for example, the Symbolist writer Dmitry Merezh-

EDITH W.CLOWES

kovsky noted that the early Nietzschean Gorky, Gorky the popular prophet of the "superhuman tramp", had been superceded by a much greater writer of truly national stature./23/ In Grandmother Kashirina he saw the embodiment of an ecstatic and earthy religious feeling which, he conceded, was the religion of the future. With such high praise Gorky the artist seemed finally to have achieved mastery. He had found his own voice. However, part of his dream was to inspire action, and as the maker of a social myth and as a spiritual leader determined to realise his idea of *lichnost'* in the social context, he remained unfulfilled. His final triumph would not come until the late 1920s.

Gorky's encounter with Nietzsche's philosophy brought out the Russian author's strong mythopoetic drive. In the God-building period Gorky formulated his own myth, finding his own characteristic response to his most important philosophical mentor. It was here that he found his own concept of *tvorchestvo* by which true *lichnost'* was to evolve. The myth of world-shaping, value-giving creativity, however, remained merely the first taste of a monumental socialist culture. Gorky, like his characters, remained no more than a prophet. Although he was an outsider in his own time, he could not become one of the new people. In this sense of personal insufficiency we find a possible reason for his attraction to the early Stalinist regime and for his decision to return from Italian exile to the Soviet Union. Looking at his homeland from a distance, Gorky perhaps believed he saw in the Soviet worker the embodiment of his idea of *lichnost'*.

In 1927 he wrote an article entitled "Ten Years" in which he praised the Russian worker for his energy and creative will. He also reminded his readers of God-building:

GORKY, NIETZSCHE AND GOD-BUILDING

At one time in the period of gloomy reaction from 1907 to 1910, I called [the worker] a "God-builder", investing in this word the idea that a person, within himself and here on earth, creates and embodies the ability to create miracles which the Idealists attribute to a power that supposedly exists outside [human consciousness]. By his labour a person becomes convinced that outside his reason and will there are no miraculous powers, except the elemental forces of nature (SS: XXIV,292).

If Gorky had not fully realised the God-building dream in his art or through the Capri school, at least he was now playing the role of a prophet of Stalinist God-building. In 1928 he had the chance to act out his God-building fantasy and return to Russia as the greater-than-human "father" of Soviet culture. In this monumental setting Gorky seemed to achieve ultimate mastery over his philosophical mentor. His myth had come true in the birth of a new and "just" society in which the masses had become the creators and he himself had become *their* mentor.

NOTES

1. See, for example, B.V.Mikhailovskii, "A.M.Gor'kii i filosofiia kul't-ury, *Uchenye zapiski: trudy kafedry russkoi literatury* (MGU), 110 (1946), 3-24; B.V.Mikhailovskii, *Tvorchestvo M.Gor'kogo i mirovaia literatura* (Moscow, 1965), pp.36-7; A.A.Makarov, "Legenda o nitssheanstve A.M.Gor'kogo kak burzhuaznaia reaktsiia na rasprostranenie filosofii marksizma v Rossii", Kandidat's dissertation, University of Moscow, 1972; and N.E.Krutikova, *V nachale veka: Gor'kii i simvolisty* (Kiev, 1978).
2. Foremost among such critics has been the Hungarian, Bela Lengyel. See his "Gemeinsame Züge in der Wertung Nietzsches und Gorkis", *Acta Litteraria Academiae Scientiarum Hungaricae*, 18 (1976), 157-90; and, by the same author, *Gorkii és Nietzsche* (Budapest, 1979). See also Raimund Sesterhenn, *Das Bogostroitel'stvo bei Gor'kii und Lunačarskii bis 1909: zur ideologischen und literarischen Vorgeschichte der Parteischule von Capri* (Munich, 1982), pp.166-7, and p.209.
3. See Ann M.Lane, "Nietzsche in Russian Thought, 1890-1917", Ph.D. dissertation, University of Wisconsin, 1976, pp.560-78; Edith W.Clowes, "A Philosophy 'For All and None': The Early Reception of Friedrich Nietzsche's Thought in Russian Literature", Ph.D. dissertation, Yale University, 1981, pp.117-65; and Betty Y.Forman, "The Early Prose of Maksim Gorky, 1892-1899", Ph.D. dissertation, Harvard University, 1983, pp.17-98.

4. George L.Kline, "The 'God-Builders': Gorki and Lunacharski", in his *Religious and Anti-Religious Thought in Russia* (Chicago, 1968),pp.103-26.
5. Betty Y.Forman, "Nietzsche and Gorky in the 1890s: The Case for an Early Influence", in *Western Philosophical Systems in Russian Literature*, ed. A.Mlikotin (Los Angeles, 1979), pp.153-64.
6. Mary Louise Loe, "Gorky and Nietzsche: The Quest for a Russian Superman", in *Nietzsche in Russia*, ed. B.G.Rosenthal (Princeton; in press).
7. Sesterhenn, *op. cit.*, p.209.
8. See Clowes, *op. cit.*, pp.147-56.
9. Quoted in A.V.Lunacharskii, "Budushchee religii", *Obrazovanie*, No.10 (1907), 7.
10. See Harold Bloom, *A Map of Misreading* (Oxford, 1975), p.35.
11. Quoted in Lunacharskii, *op. cit.*, p.7.
12. Vladimir Lenin, "Partiinaia organizatsiia i partiinaia literatura", in his *Sochineniia* (Moscow, 1952), Vol.10, p.27.
13. See M.Gor'kii, *Sobranie sochinenii v 30-i tomakh* (Moscow, 1953), Vol. 23, p.344. Further references are incorporated in the text as SS + volume no. + page no. (e.g. SS: XXIII,43). References to Gorky's *Polnoe sobranie sochinenii* (Moscow, 1968-) are denoted in the text by volume no. + page no. (e.g. IX,24) and *My Childhood*, tr. R.Wilks (Harmondsworth, 1980) by Ch + page no. (e.g. Ch: 101).
14. See A.V.Lunacharskii, "Opyt literaturnoi kharakteristiki Gleba Uspenskogo", in his *Sobranie sochinenii v 8-i tomakh* (Moscow, 1964), vol.6, p.289.
15. See Arch Tait, *Lunacharsky: Poet of the Revolution (1875-1907)*, Birmingham Slavonic Monographs, No.15 (Birmingham, England, 1985), pp.34-5.
16. See A.V.Lunacharskii, *Religiia i sotsializm* (St.Petersburg, 1908), p.46.
17. For more on Lunacharsky's socialist religion see, for example, Sesterhenn, *op. cit.*, pp.60-9.
18. See W.L.Phelps, "Gorki", in his *Essays on Russian Novelists* (New York, 1911), p.219.
19. See *Arkhiv A.M.Gor'kogo*, Institut mirovoi literatury (IMLI), E.Förster-Nietzsche to A.M.Gor'kii, Weimar, March 12, 1906.
20. See *Arkhiv A.M.Gor'kogo*, (IMLI), A.M.Gor'kii to L.A.Nikiforova, March-April, 1910 (PG-rg/28/4/5).
21. See, for example, Aleksandr Voronskii, "Vstrechi i besedy s Maksimom Gor'kim", in his *Izbrannye stat'i o literature* (Moscow, 1982), pp.48-69.
22. See Friedrich Nietzsche, *Thus Spoke Zarathustra*, tr. R.J.Hollingdale (Harmondsworth, 1975), p.62.
23. D.S.Merezhkovskii, "Ne sviataia Rus'", *Russkoe slovo*, No.210 (Sept. 11, 1916), 2.

* * * * *

DEATH AND REVOLUTION:

GORKY'S "EGOR BULYCHOV AND THE OTHERS"

Robert Russell

University of Sheffield,

England

I

After many years during which he wrote no plays, Maksim Gorky turned once more to drama in the 1930s. The first play of his late cycle, *Somov and the Others* (1931), was not discovered until after his death, but his second play of the 1930s, *Egor Bulychov and the Others* (1931), was greeted with enthusiasm by theatres and audiences throughout the country and hailed as a masterpiece of Soviet drama. Along with its sequel, *Dostigaev and the Others* (1932), the second version of *Vassa Zheleznova* (1935), and the much earlier play *Enemies* (1906), which had been banned by the Tsarist censor and had received its première only in 1933, *Egor Bulychov and the Others* laid the foundation for Gorky's reputation as a theatrical innovator in the 1930s. Each of these plays is traditional in form and is set in the pre-Soviet period, yet drama critics and theorists immediately seized on them as examples of a new and specifically Soviet drama. To some extent this can be explained by the fact that Gorky's return to the theatre in the early 1930s coincided with a debate which was raging between proponents of psychological realism in modern Soviet drama, such as Alexander Afinogenov and Vladimir Kirshon, and dramatists such as Vsevolod Vishnevsky and Nikolai Pogodin. The latter maintained that Soviet drama had to be qualitatively different from that of pre-revolutionary Russia, that it should eschew individual psychology in favour of mass heroes, that the dominant dramatic style should be elevated or monumental, and that the settings chosen should be primarily exteriors rather than the interiors favoured by dramatists of the past. Those playwrights who followed Afinogenov's lead came to be known as "monumentalists"./1/ Some commentators have argued that Gorky's return to drama helped to resolve the dispute, because in his own work of this period he synthesised the essential features of both schools. His plays revealed great interest in the psychological development of individual characters, yet in his literary pronouncements he repeatedly encouraged those dramatists who sought to emphasise revolutionary romanticism in their work./2/

Of the plays written by Gorky in the 1930s, *Egor Bulychov and the Others* had the greatest immediate impact. A new play by a writer of Gorky's stature could not but be a major event in Soviet drama, and within a relatively short period after its completion it was staged by three of the country's leading theatrical companies: the Vakhtangov Theatre and the Moscow Art Theatre in the capital, and the BDT (*Bol'shoi Dramaticheskii Teatr*) in Leningrad. The Vakhtangov production received its première on 25 September, 1932, as did that of the Leningrad BDT (both productions forming part of the nationwide celebrations to mark the fortieth anniversary of Gorky's literary début), whereas the MAT version opened on 6 February, 1934./3/ There have been other notable productions, both in the 1930s and later, but the three major early productions remain the most significant, for they reveal the qualities as well as the problems inherent in Gorky's play with a clarity that later productions - which almost invariably show

DEATH AND REVOLUTION

the influence of one of the first three - do not. Through an examination of the different approaches used by the three actors who played Bulychov, and particularly through a comparison of Boris Shchukin's interpretation in the Vakhtangov production and that of Leonid Leonidov in the MAT version, it is possible to shed light on the central problems of Gorky's play: death and revolution.

The members of the Vakhtangov Theatre were naturally delighted when they heard that they were to be given the opportunity of staging a new Gorky play for the first time for many years. Yet when they first heard the play in a reading at the writer's home in the autumn of 1931, and later when they began preliminary work on it, no one in the company had any clear idea of how to approach the production. The director, Boris Zakhava, recalls:

> Almost none of us liked the play. It seemed to us all that it was non-theatrical, that it lacked action. Over the course of three acts an obstinate, mischievous man was dying and yet just couldn't get round to actually dying. It seemed that that was the entire content./4/

Only two members of the company, Pavel Antokolsky and Osvald Glazunov, expressed any enthusiasm for the play, and so they were entrusted with the production, Antokolsky as director and Glazunov in the role of Bulychov. Their efforts, however, were completely unsuccessful, and after a few rehearsals a reluctant Boris Zakhava was instructed to take over the production. After a period of intensive study he finally changed his opinion about the stage-worthiness of the play and set about his task with a sense of excitement. He asked Gorky's permission for a number of insertions and changes to be made in the text, including the reading aloud on stage of newspapers from the period immediately preceding the February Revolution.

ROBERT RUSSELL

Gorky permitted some of the suggested changes but would not write an additional scene set in the hospital which Bulychov and Pavlin visit at the beginning of the play, and he objected to a suggestion that Bulychov might show his contempt for the trappings of religion by playing cards under the icon. He agreed, however, to the reading of newspaper articles and to some re-ordering of the text, and instructed Zakhava to put as much humour as possible into the production.

The director's major decision was undoubtedly the replacement of Glazunov by Boris Shchukin in the title role. Shchukin's Bulychov was a man whose enormous physical strength and appetite for life were hardly diminished by his illness. In scene after scene Shchukin underlined Bulychov's exceptional qualities by imbuing him with a remarkable vitality which belied the seriousness of his illness. Two examples are frequently mentioned by those who participated in or saw the Vakhtangov production. In the scene in Act 2 in which Bulychov quarrels violently with the Abbess Melaniia, he suddenly picks up her discarded staff and uses it as a billiard cue; and later in the same scene, as part of his challenge to Melaniia and to imminent death, he suddenly breaks into a dance with a reckless abandon that expresses a central feature of his nature.

Shchukin's vigorously physical Bulychov did not meet with universal approval. The Leningrad actor, Nikolai Monakhov, for example, wrote of it: "I maintain that at the stage of Bulychov's illness reached in Act 2, not only would he be physically incapable of dancing, but also even of moving quickly"./5/ Gorky, too, had his doubts about the likelihood of Bulychov being quite so lively as Shchukin made him, but he was won over to an acceptance of the actor's interpretation since he agreed with Shchukin's

DEATH AND REVOLUTION

broad concept of the role, and so he allowed the dance to remain, asking only that it be reduced in length./6/ Shchukin himself had no doubt that Bulychov's stature as a character could best be indicated by emphasising his extraordinary vitality. In fact, he claimed that someone suffering from cancer of the liver would feel no pain at the stages of the illness portrayed in Acts 1 and 2 and that he had had to include several indications of pain in contravention of clinical accuracy so as to reveal the character's plight to the audience./7/

In the other production of 1932, at the Leningrad BDT, Nikolai Monakhov gave an interpretation of Bulychov which differed radically from that of Shchukin. For Monakhov, the fact of Bulychov's illness was of paramount importance, and he saw the character not as a lively firebrand but as a solid oak of a man being slowly eaten away from the inside:

> As a result of this, in my interpretation of the role I make Bulychov large and heavy... I consider it not unimportant that there are three stages of the illness in the three acts of the play... It could be argued, of course, that one ought not to depict Bulychov as being so seriously ill. But I see no reason to accept that. After all, Bulychov dies at the end of the third act. A sick man can only be brought to the point of death by portraying the destruction of his organism. And that is what I do./8/

At the Moscow Art Theatre in 1934 Leonid Leonidov leant rather more towards Monakhov's interpretation of the role than to that of Shchukin. As with the Vakhtangov production, preparations for the MAT version of *Egor Bulychov and the Others* did not go smoothly, and at one point all three of the Theatre's leading actors (Moskvin and Kachalov, as well as Leonidov) were rehearsing the part of Bulychov. Leonidov summed up the difficulty of the role in the notes which he made before and during rehearsals. These show him struggling to reconcile the character's behaviour with the seriousness of his illness and the closeness of his death. For Leonidov, the philosophical and spiritual problems inherent in Bulychov's situation make it difficult to justify his blasphemous rejection of God. He rejects Shchukin's approach to the role, and attempts instead to "remove the physical strength but not the buoyancy of spirit"./9/

The different approaches of Shchukin and Leonidov have been summed up by one leading critic of Gorky's drama in this way:

> Shchukin and Leonidov set off in different directions and the choice of route determined the fate of the role. How did those directions differ from each other? Shchukin played life, Leonidov - death. Shchukin affirmed life, in spite of death. Leonidov withdrew from life, capitulating in the face of death. Shchukin passionately loved life in disregard of death. Leonidov gave himself up to death and it paralysed his love of life./10/

As the date of the MAT première drew closer, Leonidov became less and less confident that he had succeeded in holding together the conflicting elements in Bulychov's character, and although Vladimir Nemirovich-Danchenko, who had overall responsibility for the production, repeatedly praised the actor's efforts, his correspondence shows that he, too, had grave reservations about the interpretation. In a letter to Stanislavsky of February, 1934, for example, he writes:

> The thing is that, as I told you he would, Leonidov has gone off along a completely different path from the one on which I wanted to take the play. Goodness knows why, but he has decided that this is a play on the *subject of death*. On death in general. As if it even had something in common with "The Death of Ivan Il'ich". And he immediately settled on a very gloomy tone and began rehearsing Bulychov as someone weighed down and decrepit. Whereas I wanted him to be strong and unyielding. Moreover, Gorky warned us, "Please, you absolutely mustn't present him as an invalid"./11/

Nemirovich-Danchenko dismisses out of hand any suggestion that there could be a link between Egor Bulychov and Tolstoy's Ivan Il'ich, yet Leonidov obviously felt that such a link existed. Moreover, he knew from his

DEATH AND REVOLUTION

contacts with Gorky that the writer was greatly interested in the dramatic possibilities of Tolstoy's story. On one occasion, after seeing the MAT dramatisation of Tolstoy's *Resurrection* in 1930, Gorky was discussing the performance with some of the actors, including Leonidov, when he announced "I would like to re-write 'The Death of Ivan Il'ich' for the stage"./12/ This apparently casual remark obviously struck Leonidov as significant, for he recalled it several years later, during rehearsals for *Egor Bulychov and the Others*, and it may well have influenced his approach to the role. Was there any sense in which Gorky's play incorporated the germ of his unrealised plan to dramatise "The Death of Ivan Il'ich" (1886)? If so, then Shchukin's famous interpretation obscured this aspect of the play, whereas Leonidov's gave it central significance.

II

The great majority of critics who have considered the question have supported the view of Nemirovich-Danchenko that comparison of *Egor Bulychov and the Others* with "The Death of Ivan Il'ich" is ill-conceived and misleading. For example, the authors of the major *History of the Soviet Theatre*, published in the 1960s by the USSR Academy of Sciences, consider that Leonidov's interpretation, with its echoes of Tolstoy's tale, erroneously links Gorky's play to a nineteenth-century philosophical tradition, whereas Shchukin's interpretation of the role, they assert, correctly identifies the innovative qualities of Gorky's drama by being directed towards the future./13/

Tolstoy's Ivan Il'ich Golovin is presented as a man who is in all respects typical of his time and class. "The story of Ivan Il'ich's life was the simplest and most ordinary, and the most terrible"./14/ Tolstoy employs a range of devices, some of them uncharacteristic of his work as a whole, to emphasise repeatedly that his hero stands as a representative figure, indistinguishable in essence from other characters in the work and from the real-life readers whom Tolstoy wishes to affect by his story./15/ Egor Bulychov, on the other hand, stands out as an extraordinary man, fundamentally different from other members of his class such as Dostigaev. Gorky makes this point initially through the title of his play, which juxtaposes Egor Bulychov to "the others". In this respect the title finally chosen is preferable to the original *On the Eve*, which would have drawn attention to the symbolic implications of the death of Bulychov, but would also have misrepresented the play, which is primarily a character study with social undertones rather than the reverse.

Through the use of free indirect discourse, Tolstoy shows that Ivan Il'ich's language is indistinguishable from that of his friends and colleagues. Egor Bulychov, on the other hand, stands out from "the others" through his language, which sparkles with pithy aphorisms expressing his impatience with the self-deception and cant of those around him. The speech of "the others" varies according to the character, ranging from Melaniia's heavily Slavonicised religious language to Zvontsov's drily legalistic phrasing. For each of them, however, language is an expression of social conformity, whether to the religious order of Abbess Melaniia or to the commercial and legal worlds of Dostigaev and Zvontsov. In the case of Bulychov, though, use of language indicates a degree of alienation from the social group to which the character ostensibly belongs. Unlike Ivan Il'ich, who was born into his class, Egor Bulychov comes from a different

DEATH AND REVOLUTION

society from the one in which he has spent his adult life. As he reminds his daughter Shura in Act 3:

> I have been living on the wrong street! I got in with the wrong people and for thirty years I've been living with strangers. That's what I don't want for you! My father hauled rafts. And look at me.../16/

Boris Shchukin drew attention to this aspect of Bulychov's character when he said: "Struggling against his class, aware of its downfall, he was nevertheless unable to leave it - his feet got stuck"./17/ Unlike Ivan Il'ich, whose career develops almost automatically, Egor Bulychov requires strength to force his way into the company of people like Dostigaev, and as a result strength is the most prized characteristic for him and a recurring motif in the play. Like some other Gorky heroes, such as Il'ia Artamonov, Bulychov directs his enormous strength and vitality towards the accumulation of money, and when his strength begins to fail he understands the futility of that choice, but is unable to follow his daughter's path towards the Revolution.

So then, Tolstoy's Ivan Il'ich and Gorky's Egor Bulychov are very different from each other: the one unexceptional, typical of his class, with no characteristic voice of his own; and the other strong, determined and individualistic.

Besides the nature of the central character, the other major difference between Tolstoy's story and Gorky's play which is frequently mentioned by commentators is the relationship between historical and fictional events. "The Death of Ivan Il'ich" is set in a particular society at a particular time, but it works as a moral and philosophical parable rather than on a socio-political level. (Although, of course, a social reading is not only possible but unavoidable, given the contrast between Ivan Il'ich and his colleagues on the one hand and the servant Gerasim on the other). In Gorky's play, though, the immediate socio-political context is of far greater importance. The subjects of political events during the winter of 1916 and spring of 1917, the growing power of Rasputin, the supposed immorality of the Empress, and above all the horrific cost of the war in human lives are never far from the characters' minds. Bulychov and Pavlin make their first entrance in Act 1 following a visit to a hospital for the wounded, and the sights he has seen there remain in Bulychov's mind and colour his speech for the remainder of the Act and indeed the rest of the play. In Act 2 Bulychov reveals that his growing preoccupation with death is not occasioned solely by his own illness, but also by what he calls "the big death" of soldiers, which the father-figures of God and the Tsar are as incapable of stopping as he is of arresting the progress of his cancer. Despite the fact that the entire action of *Egor Bulychov and the Others* takes place inside Bulychov's house, the audience is not allowed to forget for long the parallels between the dying merchant and a dying society. The play's symbolism culminates in the final scene, in which Shura hears the sound of a passing street demonstration and dashes to open the window, thereby, as it were, bringing together events inside the Bulychov household and outside in the country at large. She calls on her father to come and look, but he is too weak and can only sigh "Oh, Shura", leaving her to ensure a Bulychov involvement in the coming Revolution.

Some commentators have tended to exaggerate this important aspect of Gorky's work, even going so far as to describe the Revolution as the main hero of the play./18/ While rejecting such "vulgar sociology", others, including Zakhava, have nevertheless emphasised the significance of

DEATH AND REVOLUTION

Gorky's historicism:

> I understood that events beyond the walls of the Bulychov household were in no sense what is usually called the socio-historical background. Here such events are not background but a substantial part of the action. For the deeper we penetrate into the inner meaning of the play, the clearer it becomes that the Russian Empire ... is a major character in this work of genius./19/

III

On the evidence so far adduced there would seem to be little justification for comparing *Egor Bulychov and the Others* with "The Death of Ivan Il'ich". Given the radically different natures of the heroes and the works' differing approaches to historical events, it would appear that Leonidov's evocation of Tolstoy's story in his interpretation of the role of Bulychov was as misguided as Nemirovich-Danchenko claimed in his letter to Stanislavsky. And yet, by concentrating almost exclusively on the features of Gorky's play discussed above, critics have failed to draw attention to several parallels between the works which indicate that Gorky in all probability had Tolstoy's tale in mind when writing his play, and that the general philosophical problem of death *as such* (irrespective of historical context) forms an important part of his theme. The parallel features of the works are: the attitude of the dying man's family and colleagues; the satirical treatment of professional advisers (medical in "The Death of Ivan Il'ich" and religious in *Egor Bulychov and the Others*); and the treatment of the death of the central character as a particular instance of a universal phenomenon.

In "The Death of Ivan Il'ich", as in *Egor Bulychov and the Others*, the only characters who love and pity the dying protagonist are a servant and one of the character's children: Gerasim and Ivan Il'ich's son in one case and Glafira and Shura in the other. The wives and colleagues of the dying men think only of themselves.

At the beginning of "The Death of Ivan Il'ich" Ivan's colleagues are chatting in their office when one of them reads out a newspaper announcement of Ivan Il'ich's death. We are told that "Ivan Il'ich had been a colleague of the gentlemen gathered together here, and they all liked him". Yet within a few lines the passage continues:

> So that, on hearing of Ivan Il'ich's death, the first thought of each of the gentlemen gathered together in the office was of the possible effect that his death might have in the way of transfer or promotion for themselves or their acquaintances./20/

The hypocrisy of these people is further explored later in the work when, after visiting the relatives of the deceased, one of them hardly even attempts to disguise his pleasure. Ivan Il'ich's wife, too, views his illness and death as an inconvenience and source of pain for her personally rather than for him. "I don't know how I stood it", is her comment on Ivan Il'ich's final three days spent howling in agony./21/

In *Egor Bulychov and the Others*, too, the terminal illness of the central character is discussed by his colleagues and members of his family in terms of its impact on their own financial situation. Bashkin tells Egor's wife, Kseniia, that the doctor's diagnosis is cancer of the liver and then adds:

> Bashkin: He chose a fine time to fall ill! There's money dropping everywhere just as if it were falling through a hole in a pocket. Beggars are making thousands and he...
> Kseniia: Yes, yes! People are getting so rich (XIX,16).

With the exception of Shura and the servant Glafira, who is also his mistress, Bulychov's relatives and business associates all view his impending

DEATH AND REVOLUTION

death as an opportunity for enrichment, and they split into two hostile factions, each intent on depriving the other of the dying man's fortune.

Tolstoy reserves some of his most savage satirical comment for the "experts" in dealing with the dying - namely doctors. These pompous, self-important men treat their patients as "cases" rather than as fellow-human beings, preferring to think of them as appendixes or catarrh. When Ivan Il'ich goes to visit his doctor, he is reminded forcibly of his own attitude as a lawyer to those with whom he comes in contact professionally:

> He went. Everything was as he had expected; everything was as it always is. The waiting, and the doctor's important manner, which he was familiar with - it was the same manner that he himself adopted in court - and the sounding and listening, and the questions demanding answers that were foregone conclusions and evidently unnecessary, and the weighty look which implied you just submit to us and we'll arrange it all, we know for sure how to arrange these things, we do it in the same way for everybody, no matter who./22/

In another of his works, the play *And the Light Shines in Darkness* (1902, uncompleted), Tolstoy castigates a different set of "experts" - namely the practitioners of organised religion who use their spiritual authority to attain secular ends by coercing their parishioners into political orthodoxy./23/

Gorky, too, deals satirically with professional "experts" in religion who try to win over Egor Bulychov by appealing to fear and superstition. From Father Pavlin, who uses religion as a prop for conservative political views, to the "holy fool" Protopei, who turns out to be a charlatan, Gorky portrays a number of religious parasites who prey on the fears of ordinary people facing death. Egor Bulychov is drawn to anyone who can offer him hope, but he is too intelligent to believe in any of the professional practitioners of religion, and he dismisses them one after another. Only in the case of the trumpeter, Gavrila Uvekov, does Gorky deal more sympathetically with a charlatan. Uvekov (whose symbolic name, with its evocation of the Archangel Gabriel and the notion of eternity, delights Bulychov) earns his living by allowing seriously ill people to blow his trumpet. He claims that all illnesses are caused by wind in the stomach, and that blowing the trumpet is a cure. When challenged, he admits that "you can't live without some deception" (XIX,41), yet Bulychov warms to him, for his deception is only partly designed to obtain money. In part, he practises his trade because people find it comforting to deceive themselves, and he brings them a little hope. Like Luka in *The Lower Depths* (1902), Uvekov is an ambitious figure whom Gorky can not fully condemn, since his "consoling lies" are told out of a humane desire to make life easier.

The paradox which Tolstoy explores in "The Death of Ivan Il'ich" is expressed in the protagonist's view of the syllogism about death in a textbook of logic:

> "Caius is a man, men are mortal, and therefore Caius is mortal" had seemed to him all his life to be correct only as regards Caius, but certainly not as regards himself. As far as Caius is concerned - man in the abstract - this was perfectly just; but he was not Caius, not man in the abstract; he had always been a creature quite, quite distinct from all others./24/

The universality of death, so impeccably stated in the syllogism, seems inapplicable to the self because it is unimaginable. All of Tolstoy's artistic power is applied in this story in order to make the reader feel that Ivan Il'ich's fate will be his fate too. The particular instance is universalised. Whereas in the survey of his family life and career Ivan Il'ich had been depicted as typical of his class in every respect, now, in the process of dying, he becomes the sort of unique individual that Tolstoy

DEATH AND REVOLUTION

always excelled in creating. In this way his fate is believable as a particular instance and also as a universally applicable parable; the story of Ivan Il'ich represents Tolstoy's attempt to overcome the reader's evasion when faced with the syllogism about death.

For Gorky, as well as for Tolstoy, the syllogism about the universality of death expresses a truth which must be recognised and stated. In the last scene of the play Bulychov rails against God for allowing him to die, for until that point he has dismissed death as something that can happen only to others:

> Our Father... No, it's bad! What sort of Father are You to me if You condemn me to death? Why? Because everyone dies? Why? All right then - let everyone die! But why me? (XIX,60).

In this scene, despite its symbolic undertones of the end of capitalism in Russia, the death of Egor Bulychov is powerfully literal. Like Tolstoy before him, Gorky here forces reader and audience to consider the self-deception that lies in the common attitude to death which Bulychov expresses: it is all right for other people but not for me.

While he was working on *Egor Bulychov and the Others* Gorky became increasingly interested in certain aspects of medical science, particularly in the field of longevity./25/ In May, 1931 he was instrumental in obtaining government support for the foundation of the Institute for Experimental Medicine, where work on longevity was carried out by his friend, Academician A.D.Speransky./26/ In the last year of his life his thoughts turned from longevity to immortality, and he once asked Speransky whether it would be attainable. On being told that it would not, he expressed the hope that at least scientists would be able to tell death to go away for a hundred years or so./27/

ROBERT RUSSELL

Boris Zakhava suggests that Gorky himself may have been frightened by the implications of his treatment of the theme of death in *Egor Bulychov and the Others*. Zakhava wanted to turn the final scene into a counterpoint between the revolutionary demonstration going on in the street outside and a kind of requiem mass for the dead Bulychov taking place inside the house. His colleagues in the theatre applauded when they saw the scene in rehearsal, but Gorky protested strongly that it was never his intention to show on stage the moment of Bulychov's death, so that the arrangement of the other actors in such a way as to suggest a funeral mass was inappropriate. Zakhava comments:

> Frankly, to this day I can not understand why [Gorky would not allow the mass]. I sometimes think that there was some sort of personal reason. Undoubtedly the figure of Egor Bulychov contains a personal element; Gorky put into this character something of himself, something of his own psychology. And I wonder whether Aleksei Maksimovich thought that the mass for Egor Bulychov was his own funeral service. It seemed to me that he was frightened by this gloomy, oppressive scene./28/

IV

Given the similarities between *Egor Bulychov and the Others* and "The Death of Ivan Il'ich" discussed above, together with his personal knowledge of Gorky's interest in Tolstoy's story, it is not surprising that Leonid Leonidov should have echoed Ivan Il'ich in playing Bulychov. Yet, partly because of the acclaim accorded to Boris Shchukin's interpretation, Leonidov's reading has frequently been dismissed as misguided. This article has sought to restore the balance by showing that, while *Egor Bulychov and the Others* is undoubtedly about revolution, it is equally beyond doubt that - contrary to the opinion of Nemirovich-Danchenko - it is

DEATH AND REVOLUTION

also about "death as such".

NOTES

1. See N.Gourfinkel, "Les voies du théâtre soviètique russe", in *Le Théâtre moderne depuis la deuxième guerre mondiale*, ed. J.Jacquot (Paris, 1967), p.263.
2. See, for example, N.Balabanova, "Bor'ba Gor'kogo s naturalisticheskimi tendentsiiami v drame i ee znachenie dlia sovremennogo teatral'nogo iskusstva", in *Problemy sotsialisticheskogo realizma: sbornik vtoroi*, ed. A.Priamkov (Moscow, 1960), pp.139-95.
3. E.Grigor'eva, "*Egor Bulychov* na stsene", in *Egor Bulychov i drugie: materialy i issledovaniia*, ed. B.Bialik (Moscow, 1970), pp.357-8 (henceforth cited as *Materialy*).
4. B.Zakhava, "Piat' postanovok *Egora Bulychova*", in *Materialy*, pp.151-81 (cited passage on p.152).
5. N.Monakhov, "Moia rabota nad Egorom Bulychovym", in *Materialy*, pp.241-2 (cited passage on p.242).
6. "Zamechaniia M.Gor'kogo po spektakliu *Egor Bulychov i drugie* v Teatre imeni Evg. Vakhtangova", in *Materialy*, pp.6-10.
7. B.Shchukin, "Rabota nad Bulychovym", in *Materialy*, pp.234-9 (cited passage on p.239).
8. N.Monakhov, *Povest' o zhizni* (Leningrad, 1936), p.241. Quoted in S.Danilov, *Gor'kii na stsene* (Leningrad-Moscow, 1958), pp.113-4.
9. L.Leonidov, "Zametki o roli Egora Bulychova", in his *Vospominaniia, stat'i, besedy, perepiska, zapisnye knizhki* (Moscow, 1960), p.399.
10. Iu.Iuzovskii, *Sovetskie aktery v gor'kovskikh roliakh* (Moscow, 1964), p.250.
11. V.Nemirovich-Danchenko, *Izbrannye pis'ma v dvukh tomakh* (Moscow, 1979), Vol.2, p.412. Italics in the original.
12. Leonidov, *op. cit.*, p.169.
13. A.Anastas'ev et al., *Istoriia sovetskogo dramaticheskogo teatra* (Moscow, 1968), Vol.4, p.31.
14. L.Tolstoi, *Polnoe sobranie sochinenii*, Iubileinoe izdanie (Moscow, 1938), Vol.26, p.68.
15. For a more detailed discussion of this point, see R.Russell, "From Individual to Universal: Tolstoy's *Smert' Ivana Il'icha*", *The Modern Language Review*, 76 (1981), 629-42.
16. M.Gor'kii, *Polnoe sobranie sochinenii: khudozhestvennye proizvedeniia v dvadtsati piati tomakh* (Moscow, 1968-), Vol.19, p.50. Later references to this volume will be given in the text.
17. B.Shchukin, "Beseda v klube teatral'nykh rabotnikov 19 marta 1933 g.", in *Materialy*, pp.227-34 (cited passage on p.231).
18. S.Kastorskii, *Dramaturgiia M.Gor'kogo* (Moscow-Leningrad, 1963), p.151.
19. Zakhava, *op. cit.*, p.159. For a balanced view of the role of historical events in the play, see B.Bialik, *M.Gor'kii - dramaturg* (Moscow, 1977), pp.467-73.
20. Tolstoi, *op. cit.*, p.61.

21. *Ibid.*, p.66.
22. *Ibid.*, pp.83-4.
23. For a discussion of the similarities between *And the Light Shines in Darkness* and *Egor Bulychov and the Others*, see V.Novikov, *Tvorcheskaia laboratoriia Gor'kogo-dramaturga* (Moscow, 1976), pp.482-3.
24. Tolstoi, *op. cit.*, pp.92-3.
25. See Iu.Iuzovskii, "Dramaturgiia Gor'kogo", in M.Gor'kii, *Sobranie sochinenii v vosemnadtsati tomakh* (Moscow, 1963), Vol.17, p.483.
26. *Letopis' zhizni i tvorchestva A.M.Gor'kogo*, ed. B.A.Bialik (Moscow, 1960), Vol.4: *1930-1936*, p.118.
27. *Ibid.*, pp.565-6.
28. *Materialy*, pp.165-6.

* * * * *

GAMES TRAMPS PLAY:

MASTER AND MAN IN GORKY'S "CHELKASH"

Andrew Barratt
University of Otago,
New Zealand

"Fame is a form of incomprehension, perhaps the worst". Thus Jorge Luis Borges, in a typically succinct aphorism, captures the essence of a problem which has afflicted the study of Gorky from its beginnings to the present day. From his meteoric rise to public notice at the turn of the century until his death in 1936, Maksim Gorky captivated the popular imagination in a way that few writers in any society have ever done. The mere circumstances of his life and career were the stuff of which legends are made. His emergence from the "lower depths" of Russian society, his open involvement in political activity, his uncompromising stance with regard to the modernist movements in contemporary literature, his ambiguous role in early Soviet life, and his still more mysterious death - everything seemed destined to inspire all manner of myths and controversies, a process to which Gorky himself contributed in no small degree by his constant provocations. Nor has the myth-making process ceased with the writer's death. Just as Soviet criticism has carefully fostered and refined its favoured images of the writer as the "founder of Socialist realism" and "friend and comrade-in-arms of V.I.Lenin", so those outside the USSR have shown that an energetic iconoclasm is often at bottom little more than a disguise for an alternative iconolatry. "Gorky the anarchist", "Gorky the humanist opponent of early Bolshevism", "Gorky the supporter of

ANDREW BARRATT

Stalinism" - in these and other hypostases Aleksei Maksimovich Peshkov has been made to serve a variety of counter-mythologies.

When literary criticism becomes so entangled with political polemic, there is an obvious danger that the real object of study will disappear from sight. Such has been Gorky's fate, and if his works are to be rescued from this kind of debate, it will be necessary consciously to separate them from the legends with which they have been encrusted. The aim of this article is to suggest how such a venture might be undertaken by means of a detailed examination of "Chelkash". One of Gorky's most celebrated early short stories, and the work which marked his entry into the prestigious world of the "fat journals", it has been particularly associated with one of the most durable clichés to have attached to his name - Gorky as the "eulogist of the tramp"./1/ My approach will be to trace the cliché back to its source, to document briefly its various manifestations in subsequent criticism, and then to look carefully at the text of the story itself in the light of the readings it has generated.

*   *   *   *

The publication of "Chelkash" was not achieved without certain difficulties. Based on a real-life story told to the author by an Odessa tramp during a brief sojourn in the hospital at Nikolaev, it was written in the space of two days in autumn,1894 at the encouragement of V.G.Korolenko./2/ The latter, besides being one of the most esteemed writers of his generation, was a leading representative of the Populist movement, and together with N.K.Mikhailovsky, he edited the literary section of the prestigious

GAMES TRAMPS PLAY

"fat" journal *Russkoe bogatstvo*. On completion, the story was duly read to Korolenko, who immediately recommended that Gorky submit the work to Mikhailovsky for publication in the journal. It was here that the problems began, for Mikhailovsky did not share his colleague's enthusiasm for the young author's work. In the letter he wrote to Gorky on returning the manuscript, he expressed his dissatisfaction with the story, finding particular fault with the depiction of the peasant Gavrila./3/ Although Mikhailovsky's criticism was confined ostensibly to the story's literary shortcomings, there can be little question that his doubts were at root ideological and that he considered "Chelkash" unsuitable for a journal of Populist orientation. But Gorky and Korolenko were not to be deterred. The story was resubmitted in a somewhat altered form, and Mikhailovsky presumably felt it best to back down. In any case, "Chelkash" duly appeared in the June, 1895 issue of *Russkoe bogatstvo*.

None of the foregoing would merit detailed attention had Mikhailovsky not come to write a lengthy two-part review of Gorky's *Sketches and Tales* on their appearance in 1898./4/ By far the most solid of the contemporary responses to the publication which marked Gorky's proper arrival on the national literary scene, this was also the most influential./5/ The first part of Mikhailovsky's review began, significantly enough, with a fairly detailed discussion of "Chelkash". (Gorky had also accorded the story pride of place by putting it first in the two-volume collection). Although he was prepared to acknowledge "Chelkash" as "one of the best stories" to have been produced by "Mr Gorky" (M: IX,57), Mikhailovsky nevertheless proceeded in no uncertain manner to vent his annoyance with a work in which he detected signs of a growing tendency among contemporary writers to denigrate the Russian peasant. What caused the critic particular displeasure, however, was the contrastive method of characterisation by which this denigration was achieved. Complaining first of the author's evident predisposition towards the story's eponymous hero, who had been endowed with a "certain poetic aureole" (M: IX,59), Mikhailovsky concluded his critique as follows: "Such is the tramp Grishka Chelkash. By comparison with the good-hearted, hard-working and simple peasant Gavrila, he - a thief and a drunk - is a real hero and a knight of honour" (M: IX,60).

Mikhailovsky's reading of "Chelkash" was obviously the product of his Populist sympathies (and also, one suspects, of his recent failure to deny the story a place on the pages of *Russkoe bogatstvo*). Yet the interpretation which it advanced exerted an enormous influence on critics of every political hue. The appeal of his approach lay not in its ideological position but in its method of analysis. For by emphasising the binary opposition (Chelkash vs. Gavrila) at work in the story, Mikhailovsky provided a model of the most extreme flexibility and one which was capable of expressing almost any political opinion. Thus a certain F.Dobronravov (how appropriate the name!) complained of Gorky's tendency in the figure of Chelkash to glorify "immoral parasites created by the cultural centres from all sorts of city refuse and unfit garbage from the villages"./6/ The simple shift of emphasis from the negative side of the opposition (the denigration of the peasant) to the positive (the apology of the anti-social tramp) was all that was needed for the Populist argument to be displaced by a conservative one. Likewise, Soviet critics, despite their concern to stress the limitations of Mikhailovsky's ideological stance, have nevertheless worked most comfortably within the same intellectual

GAMES TRAMPS PLAY

framework. I.M.Nefedova, for example, in a recent biographical study of Gorky, presents "Chelkash" to her readers as a story which shows "the superiority of the tramp over the bourgeois"./7/ B.Bialik, too, finds that the point of the clash of characters is to expose Gavrila's "egoistic, self-seeking aspirations"./8/ Most interesting here is the shift in the *terms* of the conflict: Mikhailovsky's opposition of tramp and peasant has been converted into a statement about "bourgeois" attitudes, which neatly avoids the issue of Gorky's notoriously hostile attitude to the peasantry, still a source of considerable embarrassment to critics in the Soviet Union. The same binary scheme (albeit with a very different interpretative focus) is also to be found in the work of Gorky's non-Soviet critics. From Alexander Kaun's statement that "the author's sympathies are obviously on the side of Chelkash, the tramp and the rowdy who has nothing but contempt for the slaves of 'honest labour'",/9/ through Dan Levin's description of Gorky's tramp as a "man of protest", a "knight of old in modern rags",/10/ to F.M.Borras' assertion that the author "was striving to present an amoral, restless vagrant [...] as an heroic symbol of ideal human behaviour",/11/ Mikhailovsky's original approach has more than proved its durability.

That "Chelkash" should have inspired so many different readings would hardly seem a matter for much surprise or concern. Indeed, it might be argued that the story's capacity to prompt such varied interpretations is a mark of its fundamental ambiguity. What will be suggested here, however, is that these alternative views have been inspired not by a careful engagement with Gorky's text, but rather by the unthinking adoption of a conveniently flexible critical strategy. What is more, it can be demonstrated that in a most important sense these readings evade the real difficulty of the story. For all their differences of emphasis and evaluation, each of the interpretations canvassed above proceeds from an identical premise - that Chelkash is the "hero", and Gavrila the "anti-hero" of the piece. The present analysis will suggest, however, that the ambiguity of "Chelkash" can only be appreciated properly if we are prepared to probe beyond this initial assumption and examine the way in which it is undermined *by the story itself.* Amongst Western writers, Irwin Weil alone has indicated the need for such an endeavour. Although his own reading of "Chelkash" is founded on the perception of its "central contrast" between "strong and weak wills" (yet another variation on the binary theme), he points out that this contrast is not absolute and that Chelkash's attitude to Gavrila is less straightforward than has commonly been assumed, mentioning in particular the occasions on which Gavrila's stories about his life in the village seem to stir a sort of nostalgia in the tramp./12/ But this is only to chip at the edifice, and Weil retreats before any real structural damage is done.

There is a need, then, for a more thorough job of demolition. By a curious irony, the one critic whose work offers the greatest support for this type of venture is none other than Mikhailovsky himself. Despite his initial insistence upon a simple "contrastive" reading of "Chelkash", the Populist writer proceeded in the remainder of his review to offer a far more subtle interpretation of the competing impulses present in Gorky's work. His most important (and, unfortunately, neglected) insight was the discovery of a tension within many of Gorky's characters between their "love of freedom" (*svobodoliubie*) and their "depravity" (*porochnost'*) (M:

GAMES TRAMPS PLAY

IX,59). "All his favourite heroes are 'depraved'", he wrote later in the same article, "even the former peasant Chelkash is a 'cynic'" [the term is one of Gorky's own, AB] (M: IX,64). In his second article, Mikhailovsky expanded further on the nature of Chelkash's "depravity", noting in particular the unhealthy satisfaction which the tramp derives from the power he wields over Gavrila (M: X,74-5). The perspicacity of these scattered remarks was later confirmed indirectly by Gorky himself. In a famous letter of December, 1910 to P.Kh.Maksimov, the writer wrote as follows of the general philosophy behind his early tramp stories:

> Of course, I never invited anyone to "go to the tramps", but I did love and I still do love people who are active and vigorous, who value and adorn life, even if only by a little, by a small something, if only by the dream of a better life. In general, the Russian tramp is a phenomenon more terrible than I succeeded in saying; this man is terrible first and foremost in his implacable despair and in the fact that he negates himself, expels himself from life./13/

Most striking here (the initial anti-Populist jibe notwithstanding) is the unmistakable ambiguity of Gorky's attitude to the tramp, the man whose "implacable despair" expels him from the very life he "adorns". But in his suggestion that he had failed properly to capture that ambiguity in his early works, Gorky was being less than fair to himself. If the failure lay anywhere, it was not with the writer but with his critics. With this in mind, let us now turn to "Chelkash" itself.

*   *   *   *

Lest it be thought from the above discussion that I wish to discount entirely the approach via binary oppositions, it will be as well to begin by rehearsing these arguments a little more fully. That Gorky invites us to view Chelkash and Gavrila as antitheses cannot seriously be denied. In social terms both men are recognisably victims of the economic times. Like Chelkash before him, Gavrila is a peasant who has been obliged to leave his native village in search of an income. But despite the basic similarity of their circumstances, the two could hardly be more different in experience, temperament or outlook. Chelkash is an habitual criminal who derives considerable personal satisfaction from the mere act of defying authority; Gavrila is participating in his first crime solely out of the desperation of unemployment. Chelkash has no long-term objective, and his ill-gotten gains are usually quickly spent on wine, women and song; for Gavrila money is the means to a clearly conceived goal of self-enrichment and security within village society. Chelkash is a man hardened by experience; Gavrila is still all blue-eyed innocence (his eyes actually *are* blue).

The differences also extend to character, Chelkash's devil-may-care bravery contrasting with Gavrila's craven cowardice. This opposition is not only obvious, but also in each instance detrimental to Gavrila's image. At every turn, the story seems deliberately engineered to bring out the very worst in the peasant lad. We are invited to witness a series of interactions in which his own part is increasingly degrading: he cowers in the bottom of the boat as Chelkash negotiates the police and customs cordon; he grovels at Chelkash's feet in the hope of receiving his money; and, too fearful to risk a direct confrontation when deprived of the money he desires, he is reduced to the cowardly expedient of hurling a rock at Chelkash when the tramp's back is turned.

In short, then, the comparison of Chelkash and Gavrila is on all counts

GAMES TRAMPS PLAY

unfavourable to the latter. But it would be wrong to think that in any of the cases mentioned above this involves the *positive glorification* of Chelkash: it is rather that, in Gavrila's company, the tramp will appear to be the superior partner more or less by default. There is, however, one significant exception to this rule and it concerns the responsiveness of the two men to the natural world. As they make their way across the dark waters to the boat from which they will steal, Chelkash sinks into a contemplative state. The sight of water, clouds and stars uplifts his soul, and the "soft sound" of the sea's "sleepy breath" arouses "powerful dreams". The passage continues: "He, the thief, loved the sea. His turbulent, nervous nature, greedy for impressions, was never sated by the contemplation of this dark expanse, endless, free and powerful" (II,21). Although here, too, Gorky ensures that Chelkash compares most favourably with the unfortunate Gavrila, in whom the sea inspires only fear (II,20), this is the one occasion on which the tramp displays a positive attribute that seems immune from suspicion. On this point, at least, we probably would not hesitate to agree with Nefedova when she writes that "as a man Chelkash stands higher and is spiritually richer than Gavrila"./14/

But this is to run ahead. On the basis of what we have seen so far, there would appear to be ample support for Borras' suggestion that "Chelkash" is little more than a well-told parable in which the two central characters are merely the embodiment of two opposite principles./15/ This opinion gains further credence when the story is viewed in the context of another celebrated early work, "The Song of the Falcon" which, like "Chelkash" itself, was written in 1894 and published in 1895. The similarity between this allegory - which turns on the opposition between

ANDREW BARRATT

the daring falcon soaring high in the sky and the pitiful grass-snake condemned to a lowly terrestrial existence - and the clash of principles at work in "Chelkash", is obvious. The connection becomes all the more intriguing and insistent when one notes that one of the key motifs attaching to Chelkash is that of the *bird of prey* (e.g. "he was distinguished from the other tramps by his resemblance to a *hawk of the steppe*" (II,9)). But though it is true that Gorky was often vulnerable to the lure of allegorical thinking, especially in his early years, the process of translating the pure images of allegory into the living characters of his short stories and plays was never simple and, as often as not, led to ambiguity and paradox./16/ In this respect, the case of "Chelkash" may be considered exemplary.

*   *   *   *

The abiding attraction of the kind of reading considered above probably tells us more about the nature of much modern criticism than it does about Gorky. The point has been well made by Northrop Frye. In his essay "The Road of Excess", Frye writes: "In our day the prevailing attitude to fiction is overwhelmingly thematic. Even as early as Dickens we often feel that the plot, when it is a matter of implausible mysteries unconvincingly revealed, is something superimposed on the real narrative, which is more like a procession of characters"./17/ The implication, of course, is that close attention to the plot of fictional works will be rewarded by an understanding rather more satisfactory than that supplied by "thematic" criticism. If we rise to this challenge by inspecting the plot of "Chelkash", what do we find? In the broadest terms, the story tells of a trans-

GAMES TRAMPS PLAY

action. Its details are easily summarised. Chelkash has run short of funds and seeks to remedy the situation in his customary manner by performing a robbery. On learning that his usual accomplice has been injured and is therefore unfit for duty, he is obliged to find someone else to perform the task. By chance he encounters Gavrila, an itinerant peasant down on his luck. The two men strike a deal, Gavrila being sufficiently desperate for employment not to enquire too carefully into the nature of the job to be done. After a visit to a tavern the men commit the crime, evade the law enforcement authorities and dispose of the stolen property. It then only remains for them to share out the proceeds in line with their agreement. Chelkash pays Gavrila forty roubles, but the peasant is greedy for more. After an altercation in which Chelkash sustains a head injury, Gavrila leaves with the bulk of the money.

On the face of it, this would seem to be unremarkable enough. Chelkash and Gavrila engage in a straightforward (albeit illegal) business deal in which Chelkash is the master (*khoziain*) and Gavrila his man (*rabotnik*). But are things really so simple? The summary, although it succeeds in capturing the story's surface logic, nevertheless manages to raise some awkward questions. The greatest difficulty surrounds the scene of the pay-off. To reduce the complex interaction between the two men in this culminal episode so that it appears to be a mere argument over money is to ignore too much. The more one looks at this scene the more obvious it becomes that behind the ostensible motives for their clash lie deeper psychological impulses of which they are unaware. The importance of this movement should not be underestimated, as it represents nothing less than a total disruption of the apparent narrative logic: at this point, we are finally brought to realise that the transaction between the two men demands to be understood not in the literal business sense at all but in the metaphorical sense that is the basis of modern transactional analysis; Chelkash's "deal" with Gavrila will only make proper sense if it is seen as an excuse for them to play a *psychological* game of *"khoziain"* and *"rabotnik"*./18/

That Chelkash's relationship with Gavrila is governed by motives other than the pragmatic need to achieve his particular short-term goal is in fact something that we might have suspected from the very outset. Consider the circumstances surrounding Gavrila's recruitment. From the purely practical point of view it is far from clear why Chelkash should have chosen to hire the peasant at all. In the course of their brief conversation he discovers very little about Gavrila except that he is a naive and inexperienced peasant lad - and hence a person unsuited both by temperament and background for the rigours of criminal life. Chelkash himself appears only too well aware of this fact. After their first exchange, he falls silent: "A vague, irritating feeling welled up somewhere deep within him, preventing him from concentrating and thinking over what had to be done that night" (II,15). As yet there is no sign that Chelkash has even countenanced the possibility of hiring Gavrila's services; if anything, his encounter with the peasant is experienced at this point only as a *hindrance* to the job at hand. Yet, within the space of half a page, it is this same Gavrila who is offered employment. This is curious, to say the least. But even odder still is Chelkash's subsequent behaviour in the tavern, where he proceeds to get his new man so drunk as to impair almost completely his already dubious capacity for successful action.

GAMES TRAMPS PLAY

Judged by any normal standards, Chelkash's behaviour here is as perverse as it is impulsive. In order to discover why he should have been moved to act as he does, we must look more closely at the dynamics of his interaction with Gavrila. From the start, Chelkash's attitude to his future accomplice is deliberately provocative. Even before a word passes between them, Chelkash pokes out his tongue at the lad and pulls a "fearsome face" (II,12). This sets the tone for what is to come. Sensing the good sport to be had, Chelkash sets out to bait the literal-minded peasant and is duly rewarded by his predictable reactions. But what begins as a rather harmless (although hardly good-natured) jest suddenly becomes more serious when Gavrila innocently refers to the free life-style enjoyed by fishermen. No sooner is the word "free" out of his mouth than Chelkash's playfulness turns to open aggression: "What's freedom to you?... Do *you* really have any love for freedom?" (II,14). The change of mood marks a critical moment in the relationship: what has happened is that Gavrila has unwittingly issued a challenge to his interlocutor. Until this moment, he had unconsciously adopted the inferior role in the game of domination that Chelkash had set up. But the mention of freedom threatens this relationship. "It is always unpleasant", Gorky explains a little later, "to see that a person whom you consider worse and lower than yourself loves or hates the same thing as you and so comes to resemble you" (II,16). The danger soon passes, however. Gavrila's response to the hostile question satisfies Chelkash that he really does have no conception of freedom and, pausing only to bait him once again and revile him as a fool, he settles back into his previous complacency.

As far as Chelkash is concerned, his game with Gavrila is already over at this point. Having established his superiority in his own terms ("I am a free man, whilst you are a narrow-minded peasant"), he indulges in a little self-satisfied whistling. But Gavrila has other ideas. Obviously stung by Chelkash's crude outburst, "the lad wanted to get even with him", Gorky tells us. Revealing that he, too, has the ability to offend when the mood takes him, he turns on Chelkash: "Hey you, fisherman! Do you often hit the bottle?" (II,15). Nothing could be better calculated to wound Chelkash, to whom this taunt represents a double challenge. It is not only that Gavrila's words signal his unwillingness to abide by the rules of Chelkash's game; by referring to the tramp's predilection for alcohol they also remind him of an unpleasant truth from which his game-playing may be seen as an escape. For all his talk about freedom, Chelkash is at bottom really only a good-for-nothing drunk. Quite unwittingly, therefore, Gavrila has placed him in a most awkward position. With his superiority exposed to the direst threat, Chelkash senses that nothing short of an existential demonstration will be sufficient to reassert his power. This he achieves by exploiting the best means at his disposal: he offers Gavrila paid employment.

The promise of money is, as Chelkash realises full well, a most powerful inducement for the peasant. Yet Gavrila does not succumb immediately. Suspicious in the first place about the sort of work that Chelkash might have in mind for him, he is further unsettled by the other's violent overreaction to this brief resistance on his part. But in the ensuing battle of wills it is, inevitably, Chelkash who proves the stronger. Moved perhaps in equal measure by the desire for money and the fear of physical attack from his aspiring employer, Gavrila accedes to Chelkash's wish. The

GAMES TRAMPS PLAY

psychological significance of this moment is marked by the appearance of the all-important word *khoziain*: "The lad looked at Chelkash and sensed *the master* in him" (II,16). The game has been resumed, but this time at a much greater level of intensity./19/ The point is driven home by the subsequent repetition of the key word in one of several passages where the narrative acquires a distinctly mocking tone towards Chelkash. The two men set off for the tavern, we are told, "Chelkash *with the important mien of the master*, twisting his moustache, the lad with an expression of total willingness to submit, but nevertheless full of mistrust and fear"(II,17).

Chelkash's game of "*khoziain*" and "*rabotnik*" demands more of Gavrila than mere submission, however. If he is fully to enjoy his superiority, Chelkash will accept nothing short of the complete *humiliation* of his man. This is where the tavern comes in. That Chelkash should first exercise his control as "master" by getting Gavrila drunk is grimly appropriate. What better way to avenge the slight of Gavrila's scornful "Do you often hit the bottle?" than by reducing him to a drunken state? Chelkash's words to the intoxicated peasant bring out perfectly the perversity of his act: "You're blotto!.. Ekh, you soppy fool! On five glasses! How are you going to work now?" (II,18). Striking first of all for the inverted logic which transforms Chelkash's drinking problem into a source of strength rather than weakness ("it takes more than five glasses to get *me* drunk"), the final question reflects more upon the tramp than the peasant. Is self-assertion really so important to him that he is prepared to jeopardise the forthcoming mission in its name?

*   *   *   *

ANDREW BARRATT

Chelkash's disregard for pragmatic considerations is equally evident during the crime itself. As the two men take their nocturnal boat trip, he misses no opportunity of aggravating the peasant's anxiety. On this point, the narrative is quite explicit: "The lad's fear amused him and he took pleasure both in Gavrila's fear and in the fact that he, Chelkash, was such an awesome man" (II,22). The patronising tone of the narrative is unmistakable, and on the very same page it gives way to one of Gorky's finest ironies. When Gavrila at last learns for certain that he has not been taken out for some night fishing, there is the following exchange:

"This is a shady business, brother... Let me go, for God's sake!.. What do you need me for?.. Eh?.. Please..."
"Shut up! If I didn't need you, I wouldn't have brought you. Understood?.. Then shut up!" (II,22)

Chelkash's admission of his "need" for Gavrila is tellingly ambiguous. The peasant, of course, is no more able to understand the real nature of this need than Chelkash is able to articulate it. But the reader is left in no doubt. When the job is done, we read: "Chelkash was pleased with his success, with himself, and with the lad whom he had so frightened and *transformed into his slave*" (II,25). By a most fortunate confluence of circumstances, the pragmatic venture and the psychological game have worked towards a harmonious conclusion. No wonder Chelkash is so happy with his lot.

Chelkash's self-satisfaction is destined to be rather short-lived, however. The problem is that his humiliation of Gavrila has been so successful that he unwittingly undermines the game at its most important point - the pay-off. The act of payment offers Chelkash the promise of total psychological gratification. The transfer of the money is intended both as the final assertion of power and a convincing demonstration of Gavrila's

GAMES TRAMPS PLAY

inferiority: by accepting payment, the peasant will "prove" that he is motivated only by brute greed. But Chelkash has miscalculated badly. By now Gavrila has been reduced to such an abject condition that he has abandoned all thought of material reward. When Chelkash opens up the final move in the game by reminding Gavrila of the substantial recompense that awaits him, the peasant responds with the startling news: "I don't want anything. Just get me back to dry land" (II,28). For the pragmatist this would be cause for celebration - after all, Gavrila is in effect putting money back in his master's pocket - but for Chelkash it is a matter of the deepest concern. Without realising it, Gavrila has signalled his refusal to participate any further in the psychological game. So again Chelkash has to resort to desperate action. Aware now that the successful outcome of the game depends entirely upon his ability to revive the "greedy peasant" in Gavrila, he immediately adopts the role of tempter. Priming him first with a reminder of life back in the village, he then plays his trump card: he tells Gavrila that he stands to make at least 500 roubles from the night's work. That Chelkash should be moved to make such a foolhardy confession is the mark of his desperation.

For all its perversity, though, Chelkash's tactic is a sure one. When it comes to the actual pay-out the following morning, it is clear from Gavrila's over-anxious opening gambit ("Well, how much did you get?" (II,34)) that Chelkash has the peasant lad where he wants him, and he pushes home his advantage with merciless thoroughness. He shows Gavrila the entire proceeds from the crime before offering him a niggardly 40 roubles; and to the peasant's wistful thought of what could be done with the larger sum, he responds with the melodramatic gesture of rustling the banknotes in his pocket. Against such a battery of provocations Gavrila has no defence; he falls at Chelkash's feet and begs him for the rest of the money. This is Chelkash's finest hour. It only remains for him to put the final touch to his virtuoso performance by hurling the money in the face of the "greedy peasant" and striding off in triumph. But, as before, Chelkash's success also contains the seed of his downfall. Even as he grovels at his master's feet, Gavrila's self-abasement is unwittingly transformed into a challenge. The very form of his supplication contains a most untimely reminder of the truth that the game had been designed to avoid. What use is money to you anyway, Gavrila argues: "After all, you're a goner... You've got no place to go..." (II,37).

Gavrila's unconscious defiance is completely unexpected and its impact upon Chelkash is correspondingly devastating. "Frightened, amazed and embittered", he is so disarmed that he can do nothing except proceed with his game plan as if nothing had happened. Uttering the contemptuous "Here, eat this!", he hurls the banknotes at Gavrila. "And, having thrown the money", the narrative continues, "he felt himself to be a hero" (II,37). Gorky's desire to prick the bubble of Chelkash's self-image is nowhere more evident, and the same impulse is equally apparent in the sequel: Chelkash's "consciousness of his own freedom" and his pride that he "would never become like that" (i.e. like Gavrila) are a transparently tenuous attempt to assert a completely imaginary superiority. But Chelkash's determination to cling to his illusory victory will withstand only so much pressure from reality. The breaking point comes almost immediately, when Gavrila, in his most striking display of incompetent gamesmanship, tells Chelkash how he had thought of hitting him on the head and pushing him

GAMES TRAMPS PLAY

over the side of the boat, a confession which he caps with a second assertion of the latter's worthlessness. Speaking of his master in the third person, he says: "He's of no use on earth! Who would stand up for him?" (II,38). Such insubordination is more than Chelkash can bear. Denied the psychological gratification which made the game worthwhile, he now abandons it altogether by grabbing back the money with which it was to be played. If you don't abide by my rules, Chelkash is saying, you can't expect to keep your winnings. But again he misjudges Gavrila badly. By now utterly bemused by the rapidity and seeming arbitrariness with which he first gained then lost the money for which he abased himself, the peasant is impelled by sheer frustration to hurl the rock at his tormentor.

Although Gavrila's attack on his erstwhile master marks the final violent disruption of Chelkash's game, this is not the end of their absurd drama of inauthentic behaviour. For no sooner has Gavrila quit the scene of the altercation than he returns. The circumstances are richly suggestive of the conflicting impulses to which he is prey. Moved in the first place to escape as quickly as possible from what he imagines to be the site of Chelkash's murder, he is lured back by the thought of the money which is simply there for the taking. But as he turns the body over to remove the money, he discovers that Chelkash is not dead, merely injured. The shock of this discovery is such that it induces not only a natural timidity but also an act of *self-deception* on Gavrila's part. As Chelkash harangues him in a state of dazed indignation, Gavrila makes the following appeal: "Remove the sin from my soul!" (II,39). To the reader this will appear an obvious ploy: by pleading for forgiveness, Gavrila is deflecting attention from the real urge that has inspired his return. It is an attempt, that is, to display that he is not at all the "greedy peasant", but rather a man moved to contrition as a result of his violent act.

Chelkash is for the moment in no position to understand the real import of Gavrila's plea. Still to recover from his injury, and (more importantly) unaware that the money is still on his person, all he can manage is a re-enactment of the final scene of the abandoned game: "'Ptah!', Chelkash spat into the wide-open eyes of his *man*" (II,39). (Note that the key word *rabotnik*, which has been delayed for so long, at last appears in the scene where the deeper significance of the Chelkash-Gavrila relationship is made plain). As his senses begin fully to return, however, Chelkash suddenly suspects that his crude gesture towards self-assertion may not have been so hopeless after all. The discovery that the money has not been taken is, therefore, a moment of triumph. Knowing full well that greed must have played the major part in Gavrila's return, he is able to resume the game simply by repeating his final move. Once again, therefore, he hurls the money at the peasant, allowing himself the further luxury of a contemptuous "Take it and go!" (II,39).

Chelkash's words signal the final showdown between the two men. Chelkash wants Gavrila to take the money and hence to prove himself the inferior "greedy peasant" once and for all. But Gavrila now has a stronger incentive to resist this psychological move. His earlier plea ("Remove the sin from my soul!") is not only a convenient evasion; it is also a sign that his unconscious rebellion has been converted into a game of his own, and one which is quite incompatible with the game devised by Chelkash. The clash is encapsulated in Gavrila's response to the aggressive offer of money: "Forgive me!.. Then I'll take it..." (II,39). This is, in effect,

GAMES TRAMPS PLAY

a counter-condition which has the purpose of thwarting Chelkash's strategy: if Chelkash agrees to forgive Gavrila, he will allow him to evade the charge of being a "greedy peasant". But if he resists this demand, the peasant will evidently not succumb to his mercenary instinct.

What is to be done? The impasse can be broken in one of two ways: either one man must back down completely, or both of them must be prepared to compromise. In the event, the latter course proves the more attractive. Thus, each man first demonstrates his willingness to compromise by making a significant concession to the other's position. Even as he announces his counter-condition, Gavrila repeats his earlier display of abject submission by falling at Chelkash's feet. Translated into plain language, this reads: "Even though I won't play your game all the way, I will accept the role of slave". Heartened by this move, Chelkash responds in a similar manner. He encourages Gavrila to take the money by conceding the crucial point in their earlier confrontations: "Don't be ashamed that you nearly killed a man! For such men as me no inquiries are held" (II,40). (Translation: "Although I won't give you the pleasure of being forgiven, I will admit that I am just a good-for-nothing"). The gesture of appeasement on both sides is sufficient to ensure that the all-important transaction can finally take place: Gavrila picks up the money. But, as Gavrila himself is only too aware, the main issue has been evaded. Hence his unwillingness to depart without one last attempt at forcing the final victory: "And will you forgive me, brother?", he asks plaintively. On this point, however, Chelkash will not be moved: "What for? There's nothing to forgive!" is the unyielding reply (II,40). Just in case Gavrila had failed to take his meaning, he initiates their final exchange with a less direct, yet more aggressive reiteration of his position: "'Well, goodbye', said Chelkash sarcastically". The venom here resides less in the sarcastic tone than in the linguistic form of Chelkash's leave-taking: the phonetic proximity of the imperative *proshchai* to the *prosti* which was Gavrila's request for forgiveness adds a particular edge to his provocation. For his part, Gavrila can only repeat his plea. But, however feeble, this is a reminder that he, too, has not backed down over the crucial issue. Thus Chelkash's final "Never mind!" has anything but the "heroic" force he would have liked; instead, it is the last evasion which brings the sorry tale of his game-playing to a suitably lame conclusion.

*   *   *   *

The analysis conducted above suggests the need to abandon completely any interpretation of "Chelkash" which deals with the story only in terms of a simple binary opposition. More specifically, it challenges the usual assumption that the final confrontation of Chelkash and Gavrila be seen as an unqualified moral victory for the former, as is suggested, for example, by Nefedova.[20] No less importantly, it provides a particular case with which to counter the equally common charge that Gorky's fiction is weak in psychology. Tolstoy's famous judgment on his younger compatriot's tendency to "invent" psychology has been adopted rather uncritically by many Western commentators. Most notable in this respect is the suggestion by Borras that the finale of "Chelkash" is an example of such invention on Gorky's part.[21] The present reading inclines to the opposite conclusion. Far from being (as Borras describes it) an unconvincing "noble gesture" inspired by the desire to glorify the tramp-hero, Chelkash's behaviour

GAMES TRAMPS PLAY

with the money in this all-important scene is much better viewed as part of a thoroughly convincing portrayal of perverse human psychology.

To make this case is also to argue that "Chelkash" is a far more complex piece of writing than has hitherto been acknowledged. Instead of simply glorifying the tramp, the story appears to promote Chelkash's "heroic" image only the more completely to deflate it. To employ a fashionable critical idiom, the psychological dimension of the story "deconstructs" the binary opposition which informs its surface features, revealing that the apparent clash of the "free man" and the "slave" masks a real relationship of a very different sort. The result is a shift of perspective which could hardly be more radical, yet it must be stressed that it has a truly corrective effect only upon the reader's perception of Chelkash. While Gavrila will certainly be viewed a little more tolerantly - as the naive victim of a cruel game rather than as a devious egoist - his behaviour still remains a testimony to peasant narrow-mindedness and acquisitiveness. But Chelkash's much-vaunted love of freedom suffers a more devastating blow. Exposed in the first place as a convenient self-image designed to distract attention (not least his own) from his crippling lack of purpose, his very conception of liberty is shown to be faulty. For Chelkash, freedom is always freedom *from*, never freedom *for*. In this connection, it is important to inspect the source of his pride on the first occasion that he hurls the money in Gavrila's face: "Chelkash listened to his joyous sobs, looked at his face distorted by the rapture of greed and felt that he - a thief and idler, *completely cut off from his roots* - would never be so greedy or fall so low as to forget himself like this" (II,37). Ironically, it is Chelkash's very insistence on the gulf which separates him from his peasant past that leads us to suspect that he protests too much. In fact, his bizarre relationship with Gavrila may most profitably be read as the story of his continued psychological dependence upon the peasant as the means by which to assert a delusive sense of superiority. Chelkash is not free from his peasant past at all. To borrow the memorable simile employed by the prostitute Nastia in *The Lower Depths* when she wishes to unmask a similar case of psychological exploitation, Chelkash needs Gavrila as the worm needs the apple (VII,176).

All this suggests that Gorky's critique of the peasant extends much further even than Mikhailovsky was moved to suspect. In the end Chelkash and Gavrila are perhaps best seen as representing the two faces of the Russian peasantry, Chelkash's cynical nihilism being the natural, though unsavoury, consequence of his imaginary escape from the traditional peasant values espoused by Gavrila. This is to make of the story one of Gorky's most negative statements on the human condition, for it speaks of a grim recognition of the immense barriers facing the achievement of true freedom.

It should not be thought, however, that Chelkash's image collapses totally before the deconstructive force of the story's psychological base. Attention has already been drawn to the lengthy passage early in the work where Chelkash responds to the beauty of the nocturnal seascape with an "expansive warm feeling" (II,21). Interesting first of all because this is a moment of transcendence which stands outside the game that Chelkash and Gavrila play, it will also remind us (especially in its reference to the "mighty dreams" stirred in the tramp's heart) of Gorky's own later expression of "love" for the tramp whose "implacable despair" is counter-

GAMES TRAMPS PLAY

balanced by the "dream of a better life" (see the letter to Maksimov quoted above). These observations lead us back to what is perhaps the most troublesome part of "Chelkash" - the prologue with which it begins.

*   *   *   *

One of Gorky's most famous (or infamous) purple patches, the prologue to "Chelkash" is a curious blend of heterogeneous elements somewhat inexpertly cemented together by the high-flown rhetoric of which Chekhov in particular was so critical./22/ It begins by invoking the symbolic opposition of land and sea. A recurrent motif in many of Gorky's early works, the emphasis here on the "grumbling" waters contained unwillingly by the granite of the harbour walls is especially reminiscent of "The Song of the Falcon", in which the freedom-loving waves sing to the glory of the bold, soaring bird ("To the madness of the brave we sing our praise" (II, 47)). The opposition is not developed here, however, and it quickly gives way to a description of the port and the lives of those who are obliged to work there. Gorky's depiction of the port's daily "hymn to Mercury" is a transparent piece of Marxist popularisation in which the literary evocation of the alienation of labour, the grotesque spectacle of man held in thrall by the very machines he has invented, slips imperceptibly into the expository language of political journalese: "They had become enslaved and depersonalised by what they had created" (II,8). However, when Gorky alludes, in the penultimate paragraph, to the "grand catastrophe" which threatens this microcosm of capitalist exploitation, the point of his prologue becomes unexpectedly more difficult to fathom. On the face of it, this might seem merely to reiterate the finale of "The Song of the Falcon" with its promise of the "revelation" (read "revolution") which is destined to come. But "Chelkash" will not yield the uncomplicated meaning of "The Song" at this point. Indeed, the revolutionary import of the incipient catastrophe is effectively annulled by the passage which describes its aftermath: "...a silence will descend on the earth, and this dusty noise, which deafens, irritates and leads to melancholy rage, will disappear, and then in the town, on the sea, and in the sky it will become calm, clear and magnificent" (II,8). It is difficult to respond to this as a vision of the post-revolutionary condition; if anything, one senses here only nostalgia for a sort of pre-industrial Nirvana.

These problems of coherence become more urgent in view of the further difficulty of explaining the prologue's specifically *introductory* function To put the matter plainly, does this prologue really belong with the narrative which follows? For Mikhailovsky, who considered this passage sufficiently important to quote it in full at the beginning of his first article (M: IX,57), the answer was clear. When he came to draw his conclusions on the novelty of Gorky's stories, he maintained not only that his heroes were by no means as new to Russian literature as many had believed, but also that an analysis of their psychology proved in the end to have little connection with the ideas expressed in the introduction to "Chelkash" (M: X,82).

Mikhailovsky puts his finger on a very real difficulty. (Indeed, he is to my knowledge the only critic to have done so). But he is perhaps guilty of overstating the case against the aesthetic and ideological unity of Gorky's story. It is, in fact, possible to relate some of the ideas expressed in the prologue to the issues raised by the following narrative.

GAMES TRAMPS PLAY

The interaction between Chelkash and Gavrila may be read quite unproblematically as a political allegory which reveals the sickness at the heart of employer-worker relations under the conditions of capitalism. Most important in this connection is the overlap between the reference to "slavish labour" (*rabskoi trud*) in the prologue (II,8) and the later description of Gavrila as Chelkash's "slave" (*rab*) (II,25). It should also be noted that there are a number of occasions on which Gorky suggests by the use of simile that Gavrila has been reduced through his labour to the function of a machine (again echoing a key motif from the prologue): "he lowered the oars into the water *mechanically*" (II,23); "Gavrila tried with all his might, working his lungs *like bellows* and his arms *like steel springs*" (II,25); "he held back, puffing *like a steam engine*" (II,25); "he rowed *like a machine*" (II,27). Another, although quite different, connection may be discerned in the crucial passage in which Chelkash's response to the nocturnal landscape is recounted. Here we learn not only of his urge for freedom, but also of the "expansive warm feeling" which offers the tramp the particular benefit that it "cleanses [his soul] of worldly filth" (II,21). As in the prologue, the libertarian spirit here merges rather suspiciously with a mere longing for a transcendent state. The story of Chelkash might, therefore, be read as a parable illustrating yet another of the dangers of contemporary life - that under such conditions the immense positive potential of man's yearning for freedom is transformed into a benign and ultimately nihilistic desire for non-being.

But, these caveats notwithstanding, Mikhailovsky's original judgment still holds good. The prologue to "Chelkash" remains a rather confused and imperfectly expressed prelude to a magnificent work which would have benefited in aesthetic coherence and thematic clarity from its exclusion. Yet much as we might wish the story to be otherwise, we should attend to the lesson which this suggests. Rather than attempt to fit the awkward details into the comfortably harmonious relationship of a "unified" reading (or, even worse, simply ignore the problem altogether), we should accept that this work, like many other Gorky products, ultimately resists the neat categorisations that critics have been determined to fix upon it. The present account suggests that "Chelkash" may perhaps best be seen as the site at which several contradictory impulses in Gorky's early art - a tendency towards allegory and parable, an as yet naively expressed Marxism, an obsessive interest in power relationships, and a deep-seated and ineradicable dislike of the Russian peasantry - are brought to a state of unstable equilibrium. Once again, it is Mikhailovsky who appears to have grasped this point the best. At the end of his review, he expressed his provisional conclusion on the young writer's achievement as follows: "It seems to me that Mr Gorky is in the grip of an idea which is not quite clear even to himself" (M: X,92).

NOTES

1. "Chelkash" was first published in *Russkoe bogatstvo*, No.6 (1895), 5-35. It was the first story by Gorky to elicit critical attention.
2. For details, see "V.G.Korolenko", in M.Gor'kii, *Polnoe sobranie sochinenii: khudozhestvennye proizvedenii v dvadtsati piati tomakh* (Moscow, 1968-), Vol.16, p.249 ff. Further references to Gorky's works are incorporated in the text, the Roman numeral indicating the volume, the Arabic the page.
3. See *M.Gor'kii: materialy i issledovaniia* (Moscow-Leningrad, 1936), Vol. 2, pp.353-4.
4. N.K.Mikhailovskii, "O g. Maksime Gor'kom i ego geroiakh", *Russkoe bogatstvo*, No.9 (1898), section II, pp.55-75; "Eshche raz o g. Maksime

GAMES TRAMPS PLAY

    Gor'kom i ego geroiakh", *ibid.*, No.10 (1898), section II, pp.61-93. All references to these articles are incorporated in the text, the Roman numeral indicating the volume, the Arabic the page - e.g. (*M*: IX,57).
5. See B.Bialik, *Sud'ba Maksima Gor'kogo* (Moscow, 1968), p.46.
6. Cited in S.V.Zaika, *M.Gor'kii i russkaia klassicheskaia literatura kontsa XIX-nachala XX veka* (Moscow, 1982), p.26.
7. I.M.Nefedova, *Maksim Gor'kii*, 2nd edn. (Leningrad, 1979), p.34.
8. Bialik, *op. cit.*, p.50.
9. A.Kaun, *Maxim Gorky and his Russia* (New York, 1968), p.144.
10. D.Levin, *Stormy Petrel: The Life and Works of Maxim Gorky* (London, 1965), p.47.
11. F.M.Borras, *Maxim Gorky the Writer: An Interpretation* (Oxford, 1967), p.70.
12. I.Weil, *Gorky: His Literary Development and Influence on Soviet Intellectual Life* (New York, 1966), pp.33-4.
13. M.Gor'kii, *Sobranie sochinenii v 30-i tomakh* (Moscow, 1955), Vol.29, p.148.
14. Nefedova, *op. cit.*, p.34.
15. Borras, *op. cit.*, p.72.
16. That Gorky's heroes are really only figures transposed from his allegories is suggested most strongly by Mikhailovsky (*M*: X,81).
17. Northrop Frye, "The Road of Excess", in his *The Stubborn Structure: Essays on Criticism and Society* (London, 1970), p.166.
18. For the best-known popular account of transactional analysis, see Eric Berne, *Games People Play* (Harmondsworth, 1964).
19. In Berne's terminology, what begins as a mere "pastime" is transformed into a "game" proper.
20. Nefedova, *op. cit.*, p.34.
21. Borras, *op. cit.*, p.70.
22. See Chekhov's letter to Gorky of 3 December, 1898, in *M.Gor'kii i A. Chekhov: sbornik materialov* (Moscow, 1951), pp.26-7.

* * * * *

NAME INDEX

In principle this index includes all personal names mentioned in the text of this book. Exceptions are Gorky himself, fictional characters and historical figures in fictional contexts. Where the title of a well-known work of fiction appears without specific mention of the author's name, a page reference is given under the author's entry.

Afinogenov, A. 145-6.
Alexander II. 1.
Andreev, L. 14, 44-5, 92, 121-2.
Andreeva, M. 39.
Antokolsky, P. 147.
Augustine, *Saint*. 79.
Babaian, E. 84.
Bal'mont, K.D. 123.
Belinsky, V.G. 135.
Béranger, P.J. de. 98.
Bervi-Flerovsky, V.V. 66.
Bialik, B. 112-14, 119, 167.
Billington, J. 78.
Bloom, H. 129.
Borges, J.L. 163.
Borras, F.M. 85, 167, 184.
Bunin, I.A. 8, 24, 74.
Byron, G.G. 98.
Charushnikov, A.P. 25.
Chekhov, A.P. 3-5, 7-8, 12, 20, 31, 41, 43-4, 46, 57, 59, 71, 74-5, 92, 98-9, 109, 111, 120, 187.
Chernyshevsky, N.G. 1, 67, 81.
Chirikov, E.N. 8.
Chitadze, G. 67-9, 78, 80.
Danko, Ia.A. 65-6.
Dickens, C. 172.
Dobroliubov, N.A. 67.
Dobronravov, F. 166.
Dorovatovsky, S.P. 25, 27-8.
Dostoevsky, F.M. 1, 7, 16, 31, 52-4, 59, 74, 81-2.
Durylin, S. 110, 112, 114, 118, 120.
Farber, L.M. 41.
Feuerbach, L.A. 131, 137, 141.
Forman, B. 128.
Fourier, C. 81.
Frye, N. 172.
Garshin, V.M. 1, 5, 7, 10-14, 23, 31, 63-104.

Glazunov, I. 147.
Goncharov, I.A. 7.
Grechnev, V.Ia. 72.
Grigorev, A. 135.
Gruzdev, I.A. 72, 99.
Heine, H. 98.
Iakubovich, P.F. 73.
Ibsen, H. 2, 57, 59.
Iuzovsky, Iu. 112, 116-18.
Ivan IV. 11.
John Chrysostom, *Saint*. 79.
Kachalov, V.I. 39, 106-07, 121, 149
Kaliuzhny, A.M. 66-7.
Karonin-Petropavlovsky, S. 72-3.
Kaun, A. 76, 167.
Kirshon, V. 145.
Klein, H. 122-3.
Kline, G. 127.
Knipper, O. 39.
Komissarzhevskaia, V.F. 106-08, 110 120.
Korolenko, V.G. 3-5, 7-8, 12, 15, 17, 20, 23-4, 31, 65, 72-4, 88, 164-5.
Kovalik, S.F. 66.
Kuprin, A.I. 74, 107.
Laing, R.D. 98.
Lenin, V.I. 130, 133, 163.
Leonidov, L. 147, 149-51, 155, 160.
Leskov, N.S. 1, 72, 74.
Levin, D. 167.
Loe, L. 128.
Loris-Melikov, M.T. 69.
Lunacharsky, A. 130-2, 134.
Maksimov, P.Kh. 74, 169, 187.
Marx, K. 137.
Merezhkovsky, D.S. 3, 5-7, 9, 31, 141-2.
Mikhailovsky, B.V. 23, 72, 89, 99, 112, 117.
Mikhailovsky, N.K. 64-5, 75, *ctd.,*

NAME INDEX

Mikhailovsky, N.K. *ctd.* 77-8, 88, 164-9, 186, 188-90.
Mirsky, D.S. 71.
Monakhov, N. 148-9.
Moskvin, I.M. 39, 149.
Nachalov, M.Ia. 65.
Nadson, S. 1, 4-5, 10, 12-14, 23, 31, 74.
Nefedova, I.M. 167, 171, 184.
Nekrasov, N.A. 67, 74.
Nemirovich-Danchenko, V.I. 52, 106, 108, 150-1, 155, 160.
Nietzsche, F. 1-2, 64, 78, 80, 83-5, 87, 127-44.
Nikiforova, L.A. 132.
Nikoladze, N.Ia. 67, 69.
Novodvorsky, A. 74.
Owen, R. 98.
Ovsianiko-Kulikovsky, D.N. 73.
Peshkova, E.P. 121.
Piatnitsky, K.P. 107, 122.
Pirandello, L. 54-5.
Pisarev, A.I. 77.
Plekhanov, G.V. 2.
Pogodin, N. 145.
Pomialovsky, N.G. 72.
Popova, O.N. 24.
Posse, V. 24, 27-8.
Pozner, V. 71.
Rasputin, G.E. 154.

Reinhardt, M. 120.
Repin, I.E. 11, 107.
Saltykov-Shchedrin, M.E. 1, 20, 72, 74, 97.
Sesterhenn, R. 128.
Shchukin, B. 147-51, 153, 160.
Shelgunov, M. 74.
Simon, J. 48.
Skitalets, S.G. 14.
Speransky, A.D. 159.
Stanislavsky, K.S. 39, 106, 150, 155.
Stirner, M. 2.
Strindberg, A. 2.
Surikov, V.I. 80.
Suvorin, A.S. 4.
Teleshov, D.N. 14.
Tolstoy, L.N. 1, 6-7, 16, 20, 31, 74, 150-3, 155-60, 184.
Turgenev, I.S. 1, 6, 8, 16.
Uspensky, G. 1, 72-4.
Vartaniants, S.A. 67-8.
Vengerov, S.A. 15.
Verlaine, P. 64.
Vishnevsky, V. 145.
Volynsky, A. 84.
Weil, I. 168.
Wells, H.G. 83, 86.
Zakhava, B. 147-8, 160
Zamiatin, E.I. 82.

* * * * *

ASTRA PRESS PUBLICATIONS

G.M.Terry.   *East European Languages and Literatures, II: A Subject and Name Index to Articles in Festschriften, Conference Proceedings and Collected Papers, 1900-1981, and Including Articles in Journals, 1978-1981.*
xxx + 218p. Perfect-sewn bound. 1982. ISBN 0-946134-00-6. £18.50 incl. p&p

S.O'Dell & N.J.L.Luker.   *Mikhail Artsybashev: A Comprehensive Bibliography*
24p. 1983. ISBN 0-946134-01-4. £1.75 incl. p&p.

G.M.Terry.   *Blaze Koneski: A Bibliography.*
24p. 1983. ISBN 0-946134-02-2. £1.75 incl. p&p.

G.M.Terry.   *East European Languages and Literatures, III: A Subject and Name Index to Articles in English-Language Journals, Festschriften, Conference Proceedings, and Collected Papers, 1982-1984.*
xviii + 152p. Perfect-sewn bound. 1985. ISBN 0-946134-05-7. £15.90 incl.

Alexander Herzen and European Culture: Proceedings of an International Symposium, Nottingham and London, 6-12th September 1982. Edited by Monica Partridge.
xii + 305p. Perfect-sewn bound. 1985. ISBN 0-946134-03-3. £14.75 incl. p&p

G.M.Terry.   *Yugoslav History: A Bibliographic Index to English-Language Articles.*
xxx + 144p. Perfect-sewn bound. 1985. ISBN 0-946134-04-9. £14.55 incl. p&p

G.M.Terry.   *Maxim Gorky in English: A Bibliography 1868-1936-1986.*
28p. 1986. ISBN 0-946134-06-5. £2.75 incl. p&p.

N.Lavrin.   *D.H.Lawrence: Nottingham Connections.*
viii + 187p. Perfect-sewn bound. 1986. ISBN 0-946134-08-1. £10.50 incl.

G.M.Terry.   *Ivan Goncharov: A Bibliography.*
25p. 1986. ISBN 0-946134-07-3. £2.75 incl. p&p.

Fifty Years On: Gorky and His Time. Edited by Nicholas Luker.
x + 194p. Perfect-sewn bound. 1987. ISBN 0-946134-09-X.

* * * * * * *